YOSLEVIN MOLINA

Chosen
Generation
From
Dust to Glory

HOW TO RELEASE THE GLORY

OF GOD IN YOUR LIFE

Chosen Generation from Dust to Glory by Yoelvin Molina
Copyright © 2022 by Yoelvin Molina.

Contact Information:
Email: MolinaYoelvin@Gmail.com
Instagram: YoelvinMolina
Youtube: Yoelvin Molina

ISBN: 978-1-7352290-5-8 (Paperback Edition)

Printed in the United States of America

Dedication

I dedicate this book to the chosen generation who are hungry and thirsty, and willing to pay the price to unleash the glory of God.

Also, to my firstborn son, Joshua Caleb, your name is a prophetic sign, and you shall be a voice among the next generation to carry on the baton and expand the kingdom of God with power and glory throughout the nations of the world.

Acknowledgments

First, I acknowledge the Holy Spirit. Without Him, I wouldn't be able to write this book. He guided and comforted me in the entire process of writing this book. Thank You for making this project possible.

Jesus, thank You for dying on the cross for me and for giving me the privilege to inherit eternal life.

Heavenly Father, thank You for creating me with a purpose on earth, and for Your amazing love. Let this book bless those who were, since eternity, designed to read it.

My wife, Clara, thank you for believing in me and always encouraging me. Thank you for your companionship. Love you, my queen.

Ricardo, I wouldn't have been able to finish this book without your help. I'm truly thankful for the numerous hours you spent with me on this project and thank you for believing in me.

Contents

Foreword

To an art connoisseur, a particular well-known artist can often be identified by the expressions, style, or even strokes that they produce on a canvas. This is because it is said that the heart of the artist will always be revealed through their art. While this observation by some is often an identifiable reality in the field of art, it is a definitive reality in the Creation of all existing matter by the Creator, God. We read in Psalm 19:1, "*The heavens declare the glory of God; And the firmament shows His handiwork.*" While an artist may seek to express a particular technique, mindset, or emotion through their work, God seeks to reveal His Glory in everything He has created! Thus, in Genesis 1:31, after He finished creating every tangible thing known to man, "*He saw everything that He had made, and indeed it was very good.*" Everything that God had created expressed His very character, His person, and His glory. God's glory can sometimes be difficult to define with a simple "word or two." It is impossible to fully define God with mere human grammatical expressions. As the author of this manuscript has done, he has himself attempted to paint a portrait of the Creator, and in particular, the unique "stamp of His Glory" that is upon the clearest created reflection of His person, the human race.

How could everything go from being "very good" in Genesis 1, to the scripture in Genesis 6:5 saying, "*Then the Lord saw that the wickedness of man was great in the earth, and that every intent of the thoughts of his heart was only evil continually*"? As you read through the chapters of this book, you will discover the sad event that produced this "coverup" of God's masterpiece. But be sure to continue the journey through until the end! You will also discover how God's glory is being systematically restored to His creation, beginning with His most prized possession and His image-bearer, man, and continuing with the Cross, the Resurrection, Pentecost, and finally the ultimate restoration of His glory in Christ's return to earth, "*The restoration of all things*" (Acts 3:21b).

Finally, I want to say how proud I am of the author, one of my sons in the faith, Yoelvin Molina. I remember the day that he stepped into the glory of God and chose to become a "Kingdom Carrier" of God's glory! That is the purpose and call of God for every person on this planet. It is His call to you! Do you hear it? Are you ready to receive it? When you do, you will begin a process of transformation in your life that will continue throughout all eternity!

> *Now the Lord is the Spirit; and where the Spirit of the Lord is, there is liberty. But we all, with unveiled face, beholding as in a mirror the glory of the Lord, are being transformed into the same image from glory to glory, just as by the Spirit of the Lord. —2 Corinthians 3:17-18*

Roger Gardner, Senior Pastor
Lighthouse Christian Fellowship

Introduction

I T ALL BEGAN IN the summer of 2018 in the living room of my apartment when I was on my knees worshiping and praying to the LORD. Suddenly, the Holy Spirit placed a word in my spirit and said to me:

> *I am forming a chosen generation out of the dust of the earth to release My glory. I will breathe life in them and form them with My own hands, and they will reveal My glory among the nations of the earth. As Jesus Christ rose from the grave, I am raising a Chosen Generation from Dust to Glory.*

Great Awakening

Jesus Christ is awakening the most powerful army across the nations of the world. We get a glimpse of this reality as we read the words of the prophet Ezekiel. In Ezekiel chapter 37, the LORD brought Ezekiel into a valley of dry bones foreshadowing the dead condition of the people of Israel. In its prophetic utterance, the LORD commands Ezekiel to prophesy to the dry bones, and immediately a great army stood on its feet. The words of this book are to awaken an army that was chosen by God from the foundation of the earth as they rise up from dust to glory!

It's Time for War

God's awakening an army because we're at war. In Joel 3:9-11, the prophet writes the following:

> ⁹ Proclaim this among the nations: Prepare for war! Wake up the mighty men, Let all the men of war draw near, Let them come up. ¹⁰ Beat your plow shares into swords and your pruning hooks into spears; Let the weak say, "I am strong." ¹¹ Assemble and come, all you nations, And gather together all around. Cause Your mighty ones to go down there, O LORD.

This war that the prophet warned us about isn't fought with missiles, airstrike, bombs, or any physical weapons. Instead, this war is fought in the heavenly realm, as our brother Paul explains in his letter to the church at Ephesus:

> For we do not wrestle against flesh and blood, but against principalities, against powers, against the rulers of the darkness of this age, against spiritual

hosts of wickedness in the heavenly places.
                                                   —Ephesians 6:12

The enemy is at work, crime is at its peak, abortion clinics are on the rise, there is a high divorce rate, and the adversarial plan of destruction is infiltrating like cancer in this generation. Meanwhile, this generation seems hopeless, dead, and without identity. Yet, the Creator is always doing His perfect work, forming a glorious generation out of the ashes of the earth. Therefore, it's time to wake up and put on the whole armor of God to bring down the kingdom of darkness, and reveal His glory.

Mount of Transfiguration

Amongst the greatest passages of Scripture is the passage about Jesus on the mount of transfiguration. There, Jesus' face shone like the sun, and His clothes became as white as snow (Matthew 17:1-3), as He beheld the glory of the Father. Can you imagine what it would be like to reflect God's glory in the same way that Jesus did? I have amazing news for you! God's plan is that His creation reflects His glory. Jesus prayed in John 17:22, *"The glory that You [Heavenly Father] gave Me [Jesus] I have given them [disciples], that they may be one just as We are one."* The glory that Jesus received from the Father is the same glory that

He made available to us, His disciples. Aren't you glad to know that Jesus Christ gave His life on the cross so you can reflect God's glory on earth? Let's consider the words of the prophet Isaiah when he penned one of the greatest promises in the Holy Scriptures:

> [1] Arise, shine; For your light has come! And the glory of the Lord is risen upon you. [2] For behold, the darkness shall cover the earth, And deep darkness the people; But the Lord will arise over you, And His glory will be seen upon you. [3] The Gentiles shall come to your light, And kings to the brightness of your rising. [5] The glory of the Lord shall be revealed, and all flesh shall see it together.
>
> —Isaiah 60:1-3; 40:5

As stated in the above scriptures, it's time to arise and shine His light, because He is ready to reveal His glory. The Hebrew word for "glory" used in the above scriptures is *kabod*, which means *honor, abundance, splendor, majesty, riches, reverence, heaviness, and weight.*[1] When the Scriptures address the glory of God, it refers to the honor of God, the abundance of God, the splendor of God, the majesty of God, and the riches of God, and so on. God's glory reveals the fullness of His nature. In my own words, I define God's glory as His greatness. In other words, God's desire is for His creation to reveal the fullness of His greatness on earth like Jesus did.

Earthen Vessel

Since ancient times, it has been common knowledge to make different kinds of earthen vessels with the mixture of clay and water. Paul refers to God's creation in a very similar manner, as earthen vessels (see 2 Corinthians 4:7). At the beginning of creation, "*God formed man of the dust of the ground*" (Genesis 2:7a). The word "formed" in Hebrew is *yasar*, which means *to form and fashion as a potter does with clay*.² God, Who represents the potter, formed man (the clay) into an earthen vessel.

A vessel is a container fabricated to hold or contain a substance. The Creator created man to be a perfect earthen vessel to hold and contain His glory. Unfortunately, after the fall, man inherited a sinful nature, causing him (God's creation) to become a marred vessel; in other words, mankind became corrupt and imperfect. Mankind was never created to have a sinful nature, but rather to be the carrier of God's glory. It was because of our sinful nature that Jesus died for us on the cross and became sin for us. Due to this ultimate sacrifice, we can once again be formed by the potter's hand (our Creator) into the perfect vessel He intended us to be.

Did you know that water is the most important element in pottery? A potter won't be able to form a vessel without constant water running around the clay. Similarly, without the Holy Spirit we're nothing but dust. Furthermore, there has to be a constant flow of the Spirit of GOD in our lives for us to be a complete vessel.

God is raising a chosen generation from the dust of the earth in order to unleash His glory over the nations of the world. However, the Lord is searching for willing vessels from amongst His people to do this. My question to you is, "Are you ready to release it?" If yes, this book will be a guide for you on how to release God's greatness in your life. Before we begin our journey to become a *Chosen Generation from Dust to Glory*, let us pray, and allow the Holy Spirit to help us through this journey:

Heavenly Father,

You have chosen me before the foundation of the earth to display Your glory, and You have given me the key to access it. I pray that You help me to unlock and unleash the glory that You have placed in me. Today, I completely surrender myself in Your hands that You may form and mold me according to Your purposes. All I ask is for my life to give glory and honor to Your name. In the precious name of Jesus Christ.

Amen

CHAPTER 1

Miracle Birth

*Yet who knows whether you come to the
kingdom for such a time as this?*

—Esther 4:14

DID YOU KNOW THAT you are a Moses here on earth?
Moses was born in one of the most critical times in
history when Pharaoh made a decree to kill all newborn
male children, and he miraculously survived. Out of all
the Israelites born in Egypt, God chose Moses to deliver
them from the Egyptian captivity. Let's look at a few of
the obstacles that Moses had to overcome after his birth:

- *He survived the massacre from Pharaoh's decree.*
- *He was hidden for three months by his mother and
survived.*

- *He survived the dangers of the Nile River after being placed in a basket, because his mother couldn't hide him any longer.*
- *He had to find favor in the sight of Pharaoh's daughter so that she could adopt him.*

Moses had one of the most miraculous births recorded in the Bible, and so did you! You may be asking yourself how your birth is comparable to

Never let the predicament of your life define who you are but let Him Who created all things define you.

Moses. For you, it all began when you became a fertilized egg in your mother's womb and were born after nine long months. You, being alive today reading this book is a miracle. Perhaps you have thought to yourself that your existence on earth was a tragic mistake. Maybe your birth wasn't planned, or you were abandoned by your parent(s). Perhaps you were born as a result of a rape, or maybe you were born with a certain health condition. I personally don't know your situation, all I know is that out of the millions of sperm that could have collided with a specific egg to form your DNA, God chose a specific combination that formed you. Therefore, never let the predicament of your life define who you are but let Him Who created all things define you. Moses was chosen to lead the people of Israel out of captivity. Likewise, you were chosen for a special assignment here on earth.

Who Chose You?

Before your existence, God had already chosen you with a specific plan for your life. In the letter to the Ephesians, Paul explains this more clearly, *"He chose us in Him before the foundation of the world"* (Ephesians 1:4). Men never choose God, rather, He chose us first(see John 15:16).

God Chose Me

When I came to Christ, I struggled for years searching for God's purpose for my life. It wasn't until one day, as I was desperately crying out in prayer to the LORD, that the Holy Spirit spoke to me and said, *"I will use you as an epistler on earth to write books."* That day, my entire life changed because I knew why I was chosen by God.

I had a very difficult time writing papers in high school and college. I was so thankful for *"Google Search,"* it saved me through many of my writing struggles. Writing became the thing I dreaded the most in school, it was my personal enemy. Every time I had to write an assignment it was like performing an insanity workout. When the word of the Lord came to me concerning writing, I took a leap of faith, believing the word that the LORD has spoken over my life, and I decided to obey it. It's only by His grace and the enabling power of the Holy

Spirit that I am able to write this book. There are many excellent writers who are more skilled than me, but the difference is in the fact that God specifically chose me and anointed me to write.

God Chose You

God always chooses imperfect vessels to release His glory. He's known to qualify the unqualified. In the Bible, there are many stories of unqualified men that became qualified by God. Let's look at some examples:

- *Moses committed murder, yet the God of mercy chose him and made him a vessel qualified to liberate the people of Israel from captivity.*
- *David was a shepherd who, according to the culture of his time, didn't have the physical characteristics of a king. However, David became God's chosen vessel, fit to become the king of Israel.*
- *Saul was known to persecute the Church in the book of Acts. In spite of that, God qualified Paul to become an apostle of Christ.*
- *Gideon was known to be the least of the tribe and greatly feared the enemy. Nevertheless, God qualified Gideon to become a man of valor.*

By the world's standards, I do not qualify to be a writer. I lack grammar skills such as knowing correct punctuation and sentence structure, to mention a few. Despite my lack of ability, God qualified me to become a writer. At the same time, God will use our imperfection to release His glory. There will be areas in your life in which you may say, *"I can't, I'm not able, or I'm incapable."* The prophet Jeremiah had the same problem. He said, *"Lord God! Behold, I cannot speak, for I am a youth"* (Jeremiah 1:6). The LORD called Jeremiah to be a prophet in one of the most tragic times in Israel's history. He felt he was too young to fulfill the role of a prophet. Yet, God doesn't see us the way man does, or the way we see ourselves. The Creator sees us the way He created us to be.

> *God always chooses imperfect vessels to release His glory.*

God Sees Man's Heart

The prophet Samuel was to anoint one of the sons of Jesse to become the next king of Israel. When the prophet Samuel saw Eliab, one of Jesse's sons, his response was as follows:

> [6] Surely the Lord's anointed is before Him! [7] But the Lord said to Samuel, "Do not look at his appearance or at his physical stature, because I have refused him. For the Lord does not see as man sees; for man looks

> at the outward appearance, but the Lord looks at the heart. —1 Samuel 16:6-7

Samuel, a man of God highly respected in Israel, first saw David's older brother, Eliab, as the son that God would choose as king, and he failed to see David as the rightful king. God sees man (His creation) in a way that is beyond what man can perceive. While man sees the outward appearance, the LORD sees our hearts. Let's always pray that the LORD may open our spiritual eyes so we may see ourselves the way God sees us and that we may become what He intended for us to become. He has an amazing plan for our lives that is greater than we can ever imagine. All we must do is yield ourselves to Him and believe in His promises over our lives.

Why Did God Choose Us?

If God didn't choose man to only perform works on earth, then why did God choose us? Let's go to John 15:16a to see what Jesus said:

> You did not choose Me, but I chose you and appointed you that you should go and bear fruit, and that your fruit should remain.

God chooses us to bear fruit, and that fruit we produce remains on earth. God created mankind to live a fruitful life. The first commandment that the LORD gave Adam was to be fruitful and multiply, then to subdue the earth (see Genesis 1:28). This indicates that you will determine the quality of the fruit in your life. Before Jesus Christ ascended to heaven, He urged his disciples to make *"disciples of all the nations"* (Matthew 28:18b). The Creator chose us before the foundation of the earth to bear fruit for His kingdom, and He chose us to bear fruit that remains for generations to come.

What Kind of Fruits Should We Produce?

What kind of fruit was Jesus referring to? Let's read Apostle Paul's letter to the Galatians' church:

> 22 But the fruit of the Spirit is love, joy, peace, long suffering, kindness, goodness, faithfulness, 23 gentleness, self-Control. Against such there is no law.
> —Galatians 5:22-23

The fruit of the Spirit is a Christ-like character, a character that reveals the holy nature of God in the Believer. When a person receives the Holy Spirit, the Spirit of God transforms them and reshapes their character through their relationship with Him.

How Do We Bear Fruit?

Jesus told us clearly what we must do—bear fruit! He said the following in John 15:4-5:

> 4 Abide in Me, and I in you. As the branch cannot bear fruit of itself, unless it abides in the vine, neither can you, unless you abide in Me. 5 "I am the vine, you are the branches. He who abides in Me, and I in him, bears much fruit; for without Me you can do nothing.

Bearing fruit in our lives comes forth by abiding in Jesus. To abide in Jesus means having an intimate relationship with Him. Maintaining our relationship with Christ will produce the fruit of His character in our lives. Our relationship with the Creator will determine the level of our transformation. Paul said the following in 2 Corinthians 3:18:

> But we all, with unveiled face, beholding as in a mirror the glory of the Lord, are being transformed into the same image from glory to glory, just as by the Spirit of the Lord.

Paul emphasizes how we are being transformed into God's image from glory to glory. The level of glory that you reveal on earth would be determined by your relationship with the LORD.

What Happens When You Bear Fruit?
Bearing fruit has everything to do with pleasing our Heavenly Father. Look what Jesus said in John 15:8:

> By this My Father is glorified, that you bear much fruit; so you will be My disciples.

Jesus told us clearly, if you deeply desire to glorify the Father, and become His disciple, then you must bear much fruit. It is in the Father's heart that His creation expands His kingdom on earth by bearing fruit.

What Happens If You Don't Bear Fruit?
So, what is the consequence of not bearing fruit? According to the Scriptures, any person who doesn't bear fruit will be cut off and thrown into the fire.

> Every tree that does not bear good fruit is cut down and thrown into the fire. —Matthew 7:19

> If anyone does not abide in Me, he is cast out as a branch and is withered; and they gather them and throw them into the fire, and they are burned.
> —John 15:6

You Will Know Them by Their Fruits

In the last days, many false ministers will come disguised in sheep's clothing, deceiving

> *Never judge a tree by its appearance, but by the fruit it bears.*

many, and the only way you may identify them is by their fruits, not by their gifts (see Matthew 7:15-16). Never judge a tree by its appearance, but by the fruit it bears.

Many will come to Jesus and say to Him, "*Lord, Lord, have we not prophesied in Your name, cast out demons in Your name, and done many wonders in Your name?*"

And the LORD will respond to them, "*I never knew You; depart from Me, you who practice lawlessness!*" (Matthew 7:22-23, paraphrased).

There is a difference between knowing about God and knowing Him. For example, there are people that know about me. They may know my name, my age, my dislikes, they may know many things about me, but the only person in the world that knows me intimately is my wife. The word "knew" in the above scripture is the Greek word "*ginosko*" which is the same word used for sexual intercourse between a man and a woman.[1] The biblical expression for sexual intercourse between husband and wife is to know. When a man knows his wife they become "one flesh" (see Genesis 2:24). Jesus prayed for all Believers to be one with the Father as He was one with Him (see John 17:20-21). This indicates that to be one with God we need to know Him intimately. There are many Believers that know about Christ but do not have an intimate relationship with Him. And, if we don't take the time to know God in our lifetime on earth, He will cast away His memory of us as in Matthew 7:22 where it says, *"I never knew you."*

Living Miracle

Remember, you're not a mistake, but you are a living miracle called for greatness. Out of all the earth's inhabitants, God designed you uniquely to reveal His glory. Having said that, you possess the right to choose your destiny.

MIRACLE BIRTH

In this chapter you learned that you are not a mistake, but you are a living miracle called for greatness. Out of all the earth's inhabitants, God designed you uniquely to reveal His glory.

REVIEW QUESTIONS

1. According to John 15:16, who chose you, and why were you chosen?

    _____

    _____

2. Read John 15:4-5. How can you bear much fruit?

    _____

    _____

3. What are the consequences of not bearing fruit? (Read Matthew 7:19; John 15:6.)

    _____

    _____

4. What happens when you bear fruit? (Read John 15:8.)

    _____

    _____

PERSONAL QUESTIONS

1. Have you ever thought of yourself as a mistake? If yes, why?

    _____

    _____

    Note: You are not a mistake, but a living miracle created for greatness. Before you were formed in your mother's womb, He had already thought of you and created you with a plan to prosper you.

2. In what areas in your life have you used the words *"I can't, I'm not able, or I'm incapable"*?

    _____

    _____

3. Read Matthew 19:26. In your own words, write why you shouldn't use the words *"I can't, I'm not able, or I'm incapable"* in your vocabulary.

    _____

    _____

4. According to the scriptures, we have learned that God created us to bear fruit. Knowing this, ask yourself this question: Am I bearing fruit for God's kingdom? If not, why?

    _____

Note: Don't feel discouraged if you aren't bearing fruit. However, feel motivated and encouraged knowing that today is a new opportunity to turn your life around and begin to bear fruit for His kingdom.

5. There are three different perceptions in a person's life: your personal perception (*the way you see yourself*), man's perception (the way others see you), and God's perception (*the way God sees you*). Briefly describe each perception in your life.

Personal Perception:

_____

_____

_____

Man's Perception:

_____

_____

_____

God's Perception:

_____

_____

_____

Note: When you look in the mirror, what do you see? Yourself. However, God doesn't see you; He sees Himself in you (see 2 Corinthians 3:17-18). Remember, man sees the outward appearance, but God sees our hearts.

Prayer Time: Let's take a moment and pray as Elijah prayed for his servant that his spiritual eyes be opened. Pray that you may see yourself as God designed you to uniquely reveal His glory (Read II King 6:17; 1 Samuel 16:7).

Heavenly Father,

I personally thank You that I'm not a mistake but a living miracle called for greatness. Father remove the scales from my eyes that blind me and keep me from revealing You to others. I pray to open my spiritual eyes so that I may see myself the way You see me. In the precious name of Jesus Christ, I pray.

Amen

CHAPTER 2

New Creation

*Therefore, if anyone is in Christ, he is a new
creation; old things have passed away; behold,
all things have become new.*

—2 Corinthians 5:17

IN THE YEAR 2012, my friend Ricardo gave his life to
Christ. In the spring of that year, he returned home
from college to visit his family. I remember that it had
been several months since I hadn't seen him. So, I went
to visit him to catch up with him. However, when I saw
him, I did not recognize him. He was a totally different
person, the way he expressed himself, and spoke was as
though I was talking to a different person. Deep in my
heart, I desired what he had, so that day, unexpectedly,
"the true Light which gives light to every man" (John 1:9)
entered the living room where we were and transformed

my whole life. On that day, I gave my life to Jesus Christ. After my experience, I understood what Paul wrote in 2 Corinthians 5:17 (see above).

According to John 3:5, the moment a Believer is born again is the moment they put on Christ and receive a new

> *The new nature will empower us to overcome the desires of the flesh.*

nature. When this happens, the person literally becomes a new creation. For example, a person is a wanted criminal in the United States for committing a crime, and the criminal deeply desires to start a new life, but due to his past life, he isn't able to. The only possible way for them to start new is if the criminal changes his identity. A new identity means a new name, fingerprint, physical appearance, voice tone, and DNA. Basically, the criminal becomes a new person. That is what happens when a person *"puts on"* Christ (the new nature), he or she becomes a new creation. The new nature enables us to walk a life in the Spirit and helps us not fulfill the lust of the flesh. Let's look at how the Apostle Paul explains it, *"But put on the Lord Jesus Christ, and make no provision for the flesh, to fulfill its lusts"* (Romans 13:14). The new nature will empower us to overcome the desires of the flesh.

Ancient Serpent

When a man walks in the flesh, he gives legal access to the enemy, but when a man walks in his new nature, he has legal

> *The enemy has no legal access over you unless God allows it.*

authority over the enemy. The apostle Paul explains it in Galatians 5:16 saying, "*Walk in the Spirit, and you shall not fulfill the lust of the flesh.*" When a man walks in the flesh, he becomes the enemy food. For example, the LORD said to the ancient serpent, "*On your belly, you shall go, And you shall eat dust all the days of your life*" (Genesis 3:14b). This verse clearly explains how man made out of the dust of the earth became the serpent's prey and food on earth. The enemy, known as the serpent in the book of Genesis, becomes the dragon in the book of Revelation (see Revelation 20:2). When a man "*puts on*" Christ, the enemy has no legal access over him life unless God allows it.

Old Nature

My old nature got me expelled from college. I suffered from stuttering problems—unable to properly speak in public, had drinking problems, hated reading and writing, and sexually lusted. Despite how sinful my old nature was, when I came to Christ, I became a new creation. The old me became buried and dead, and a new man was born. The new man graduated from college, acquired the ability to speak in public without stuttering, enjoys reading and writing, and overcame alcohol and sexual lust. You aren't the exception. The Bible says in I John 1:9, "*If we confess our sins, He is faithful and just to forgive us our sins and to cleanse us from all unrighteousness.*" Do not let your past dictate your future! In Christ, our past is erased and forgotten. The Scriptures say in Hebrews 8:12 (NIV), "*For I will forgive their wickedness and will remember their sins no more.*" God forgets our sins, but most of the time, we remind Him of our past.

Saul Encounters the True Light

God forgetting our past sins reminds me of the story of Saul on his journey to Damascus, "*A light shone around him from heaven*" (Acts 9:3b). Saul encountered the true Light that completely changed his life. In fact, Saul, who was known to persecute the Church, became the well-known, respected Apostle Paul, and instead of killing Christians or destroying and persecuting churches, he was building churches and edifying the body of Christ.

When Jesus Christ comes into a person's life, a new identity is born. The old man is buried and dead, and a new man is born and alive. Paul understood it, he tells the Galatian's church, "*I have been crucified with Christ; it is no longer I who live, but Christ lives in me*" (Galatians

2:20a). Paul was saying that the man who previously murdered and persecuted the Church is dead and a new man was birthed by the Holy Spirit. The Saul that was known to persecute the Church and kill Christians was no longer alive. Saul died, and a new man rose from the grave, and his name was Paul.

Abraham's Only Son

Abraham had a similar experience. On three different occasions, God specifically used the phrase "*your only son,*" when referring to Isaac (see Genesis 22:2, 12, 16). But doesn't the scripture say that Abraham begot another son named Ishmael? The truth is that Abraham never begot Ishmael. Abram begot Ishmael, but not Abraham. Let's now look at what the book of Genesis 16:15 says, "*So Hagar bore Abram, a son; and Abram named his son, whom Hagar bore, Ishmael.*" This scripture simply explains how Abram begot Ishmael. When Abram was ninety-nine years old, the Bible says in Genesis 17:1 that the "*LORD appeared to Abram,*" and in his encounter with the LORD, his name was changed to Abraham. Then, Abraham begot Isaac, the son of the promise. Abram begot Ishmael, rushed to obtain God's promise, died, and was born as a new spiritual man named Abraham. That is exactly what happens when a person puts on Christ, he or she becomes a new creation.

Lazarus' Resurrection

One of the most incredible miracles in the ministry of Jesus Christ was the resurrection of Lazarus. Jesus performed a number of amazing miracles such as: restoring the eyes of the blind, setting the captive-free, lame and paralytics walking, calming the storm, turning water into wine, great catch of fish, multiplication of loaves and fishes, *"and there are also many other things that Jesus did, which if they were written one by one, I suppose that even the world itself could not contain the books that would be written"* (John 21:25). In Scripture, we read of several scenarios of people raised from the dead. Let's look at the following examples:

- *The widow of Zarephath's son* (1 Kings 17:17–24)
- *The Shunammite woman's son* (2 Kings 4:18–37)
- *The widow of Nain's son* (Luke 7:11–17)
- *Jairus' daughter* (Luke 8:40–56)
- *Tabitha in the early church* (Acts 9:36–43)

Lazarus' miracle was something unique and special. The resurrection of Lazarus was the final miracle that Jesus performed on earth. Typically, the best performance is the last one, such as the last performance in a concert or the best boxing match that's held last. Lazarus was somewhat unusual; the Scriptures relate that Lazarus was dead for four days. One of the Jewish beliefs of that time was that the spirit of a deceased person remains around the body for up to three days. Science teaches that when a person dies, the internal organs of the human body begin to decompose after 24-72 hours. Therefore, Jews understood that after four days, a corpse didn't have much hope of resurrecting.

When Jesus arrived on the 4th day, Lazarus' sister Mary told Him, "Lord, if You had been here, my brother would not have died" (John 11:32). Remember the story of Martha and Mary? Mary was the one that sat at the Lord's feet listening to Him while Martha served (see Luke 10:38–42). Perhaps Mary heard about the incredible miracles, signs, and wonders of Jesus, how Jesus raised Jairus' daughter or the widow's son in Nain from the dead. I believe that for a few days after Lazarus died, Mary still had faith and believed that Jesus could raise him from the dead. However, as the days passed and Jesus didn't arrive during their own timeline, Mary and Martha began to lose hope that Lazarus would live again.

Continuing to study the story of Lazarus, we find that after he was resurrected by Jesus, he came out of the tomb in graveclothes. John's gospel says the following:

> ^{43} Now when He had said these things, He cried with a loud voice, "Lazarus, come forth!" ^{44} And he who had died came out bound hand and foot with graveclothes,

and his face was wrapped with a cloth.

—John 11:43-44

Although Lazarus was physically alive, he was bound because of the graveclothes. Jesus Christ has rescued and delivered many Believers from drug addiction, prostitution, fornication, depression, alcoholism, delinquency, and so on. However, some Believers become stagnant in their walk and are bound because they don't get rid of the graveclothes (the old nature). It's sad to know that Believers have received resurrection power through Jesus Christ and aren't willing to walk in the newness of life because they have become too comfortable with their old nature. And if this generation isn't willing to remove their death clothes, they will never release God's glory on earth.

The Resurrection of Jesus

Lazarus resurrected with his graveclothes, but Jesus Christ left His graveclothes inside the tomb (see John 20:6-7). Graveclothes don't belong on the living. Graveclothes belong on those in the grave. We must understand that we have been resurrected with Christ. Paul wrote the following in the book of Romans:

Therefore we were buried with Him through baptism into death, that just as Christ was raised from the

dead by the glory of the Father, even so we also
should walk in newness of life. —Romans 6:4

Jesus Christ paved the way so we might walk in the
newness of life and reveal the fullness of His greatness
on earth. So, what stops us from walking in the newness
of life is not the enemy, but ourselves. A generation will
never release God's glory on earth until they decide to
get rid of themself and allow Christ to reign.

Burning Bush

When God called Moses in the burning bush, He told
Moses to *"take your sandals off your feet, for the place
where you stand is holy ground"* (Exodus 3:5). Moses was
a murderer, yet his past didn't dictate his future; He
decided to remove his sandals and step into a new journey with the God. The sandals symbolize the old nature
or our past. And oftentimes, we attach ourselves to our
past, or our old nature, and become afraid or we feel
unworthy to remove our sandals. Remember, Jesus paid
the ransom for our past, present, and future, and it's our
choice if we enter the newness of life or not. It's time
for a chosen generation to remove their sandals from
their feet, leave their past behind, and begin to enter a
new journey with the God.

Before I continue, if you feel attached to sin, or the past, or anything that is disabling you to remove your sandals, this is a burning bush moment in which you cast all your cares to Jesus Christ and begin a new journey with Him. Remember, Moses was a murderer and was walking with this guilt for many years. Despite that, he made a choice to remove his sandals. I don't know your past or your struggles, however, I know the One that forgets our past and makes all things new.

Power of The Cross

In the book of the minor prophet Zechariah, Joshua was a high priest that was clothed with filthy garments before the angel of LORD. The

> *Jesus Christ provided mankind a new covering through the shedding of His blood.*

angel of the LORD removed his iniquity and clothed him with a new rich robe (see Zechariah 3:3-5). Joshua, which means "Jehovah is salvation,"[1] represents Jesus Christ, our high priest, who came to earth and clothed Himself with the iniquities and the sins of the world. After His resurrection from the dead, He was clothed with righteousness. Jesus Christ provided mankind a new covering through the shedding of His blood. We must come to completely understand the power of the cross. Jesus really meant it when He said in John 19:30, *"It is finished."* Let's look at the following verses:

- *Who Himself bore our sins in His own body on the tree, that we, having died to sins, might live for righteousness.* – 1 Peter 2:24

- *Who knew no sin to be sin for us, that we might become the righteousness of God in Him.* – 2 Corinthians 5:21

- *Christ has redeemed us from the curse of the law, having become a curse for us.* – Galatians 3:13

Two thousand years ago, Jesus bore all our sins, and we forget what Jesus did on the cross. Many times, we entangle ourselves in our past sins, allowing the enemy to build strongholds in our minds. Instead of forgetting our past, we allow our past to dictate our future. We must be careful, so we don't end up like Lot's wife as a pillar of salt (see Genesis 19). Lot's wife was so busy thinking of her past life that she forgot what lay ahead. Our brother Paul clearly understood it, he wrote in Philippians 3:13-15:

> [13] Brethren I do not count myself to have apprehended; but one thing I do, forgetting those things which are behind and reaching forward to those things which are ahead, [14] I press toward the goal for the prize of

> the upward call of God in Christ Jesus. [15] Therefore
> let us, as many as are mature, have this mind; and if
> in anything you think otherwise, God will reveal even
> this to you.

We need to learn to be Christ-minded by pressing toward our goal and not returning to our past. The Church of Christ cannot be *"conformed to this world, but* [needs to be] *transformed by the renewing of* [their] *mind, that* [they] *may prove what is that good and acceptable and perfect will of God"* (Romans 12:2, paraphrased). The Church has to be renewing their minds continually and permitting the new man to rule over it. So, we need to change our perspective and begin to see the things of the Spirit, not of the flesh. Remember, Christ sacrificed His life so that you may walk in newness of life through Him.

New Wine

In the parable of the wineskin, Jesus spoke about not pouring new wine into old wineskins because it would ruin the wineskins (see Luke 5:37-38). Our Creator desired to pour out His glory upon His creation, but unfortunately, He can't pour new wine into old wineskins. Meaning that God cannot pour His glory into us if we are continually manifesting our old nature. If we want to receive the new wine that God has in store for us, we need to walk and live in our new creation. Therefore, it is time for this chosen generation to put away their old man, and put on Christ, the new man, in order to unleash His glory.

NEW CREATION

The purpose of this chapter is to help you understand that you are a new creation in Christ, and that it is our responsibility to get rid of our old nature so we might walk in the newness of life revealing the fullness of His glory on earth.

REVIEW QUESTIONS

1. According to 2 Corinthians 5:17, what happens when you are in Christ?

   _____

   _____

   _____

2. Why is it so important to *"put on Christ"* according to Romans 13:14?

   _____

   _____

3. In the story of Lazarus found in the gospel of John 11:43-44, what prevented Lazarus from walking in the newness of life?

   _____

   _____

4. According to the account of Jesus' resurrection in John 20:6-7, where did Jesus leave His graveclothes?

_____

_____

5. How does the parable of the wineskins in Luke 5:37-38 relate to you releasing God's glory?

_____

_____

PERSONAL QUESTIONS

1. What is one of your major strugglles in your walk with Christ?

_____

_____

2. Make a list of things in your life that are preventing you from walking in the newness of life?

_____

_____

_____

3. Although Lazarus was physically alive after Jesus raised him from the dead, he was bound because of the graveclothes. Notice in John 11:43-44 the graveclothes had Lazarus bound in three parts of the body: hands (*representing God's work in your life*), feet (*representing God's destiny in your life*), and face

(*representing God's vision in your life*). Briefly describe any of the three areas in your life in which you are being bound.

Hands:

_____

_____

_____

Feet:

_____

_____

_____

Face:

_____

_____

_____

Note: The greatest enemy in our lives is not Satan, the greatest enemy is ourselves. So, what is stopping you from walking in the newness of life is not the enemy but yourself. Jesus paid the price on Calvary so mankind could inherit a new nature. However, you are responsible for getting rid of the old nature in your life. If you deeply desire to pour out God's glory in your life, then you have to get rid of the old man and begin to walk in the new.

Prayer Time: Let's take a moment and pray that the Holy Spirit reveal any binding graveclothes in your life that is preventing you from releasing God's glory in your life.

Heavenly Father,

You made me a new creation through Jesus Christ, and I desire to walk in the newness of life that You gave to me. So, today I make the decision to cast all my cares towards You because You care for me. I present myself to You as a living sacrifice. By Your grace, strength, and the empowerment of the Holy Spirit, I remove my sandals of _____, (Be specific, for example: lying, anger, resentment, guilt, lust, and so on) and today I enter a new journey with my LORD and Savior Jesus Christ. The Scripture states in the gospel of Matthew 11:28-30, "Come to Me, all you who labor and are heavy laden, and I will give you rest. Take My yoke upon you and learn from Me, for I am gentle and lowly in heart, and you will find rest for your souls. For My yoke is easy and My burden is light." Take my yoke, and my heavy burden that I may find rest in You. I thank You for today, tomorrow, and forever. I give You all the glory, honor, and praise. In the precious name of Jesus Christ.

Amen.

CHAPTER 3

Image of Man

> ^{26} *Then God said, "Let Us make man in Our image, according to Our likeness..."* ^{27} *So God created man in His own image; in the image of God He created him; male and female He created them."*
>
> **—Genesis 1:26-27**

A T THE BEGINNING OF creation, God created the earth, firmament, seas, vegetation, and everything that exists on earth with the sound of His voice. On the sixth day of creation, God formed man out of the dust of the earth. Out of all of God's creation, man became the exclusive creation, created in His image and likeness. Adam became the first human created in the image of God. After he was created, the LORD placed him in a perfect abode called the Garden of Eden, where he dwelt in the presence of God and carried His glory. He was the perfect representation of the God figure on earth, created to rule and to have dominion over the earth and over every living creature.

What Is an Image?

The Hebrew word for "image" as used in Genesis 1:26 is the word *"selem,"*[1] which comes from an unused

> *You are created to reflect the original image of God's glory on earth.*

root word *"sel,"* meaning *shadow.*[2] The Merriam-Webster dictionary defines the word "shadow" as a *reflected image.*[3] So, when God said in Genesis 1:26, *"Let Us make man in Our image,"* He simply meant (in my own words), *"I'll create man to become My shadow, or a reflected image of Myself on earth."* This implies that you are created to reflect the original image of God's glory on earth.

Facts About Shadows

A shadow cannot coexist or move without an object. For example, if an object spins, the shadow spins, or if the object moves upward or downward, the shadow moves in the same direction. Therefore, a shadow depends on an object to exist. Likewise, mankind is entirely dependent on the Creator, and without the Creator, mankind cannot exist. Without an object, there aren't any shadows, and without the Creator you don't exist.

Another interesting fact about a shadow is the distance between the light source and the object determining the size of the shadow. The nearer an object is to the light source, the larger the shadow becomes. The further an object is from the light source, the smaller the shadow. And that is exactly what occurred when man sinned against God, it brought separation between creation and the Creator. Therefore, the closer man is to the

> *The closer man is to the Creator, the greater the manifestation of His glory.*

Creator, our source of life, the greater the manifestation of God's glory he reflects on earth. It's in God's heart that His creation draws near to Him. James explains this more clearly, "*Draw near to God and He will draw near to you*" (James 4:8a). God desires His creation to reflect His glory, yet He is waiting for His creation to draw closer to Him. Drawing in closer to God means to deepen your personal relationship with Him.

Fall of Man

When Adam and Eve sinned against God, the perfect image of God that man reflected on earth became contaminated. Contamination involves something that is in a state of pureness, and by means of some sort of adulteration, it changes to a state of impureness. For instance, if I drop a small portion of dirt in a glass of clean water, would a person drink the glass of water? Of course not, but why? For the simple fact that the water has become contaminated with dirt. In a similar manner, sin has entered man and contaminated the image of man and resulted in man inheriting a sin nature.

The sin nature became mankind's stumbling block to manifesting His glory and separated man from His Creator. The good news is that Jesus Christ paved the way on the cross and demolished man's sinful nature to enable mankind to become God's shadow on earth. In this chapter I will be addressing three ways sin contaminated the original image of man.

CLOTHING

The first way sin contaminated the image of man was clothing. Clothing plays an essential role in our society by covering man and woman's nakedness.

> *The original plan of God was for His creation to clothe themselves with His glorious nature.*

People wear different types of clothing, depending on the type of weather. As the seasons change, a person may wear coats in winter, dresses in spring, shorts in summer, and long-sleeves or sweaters in autumn. The original plan of God was for His creation to clothe themselves with His glorious nature. However, the garment of perfection, righteousness, and holiness that covered man was lost after the fall of man.

Loss of Covering

Mankind is the only creation of God that wears clothing to cover their nakedness. Everything that the LORD created has its own kind of covering. For example, fishes have scales, birds have feathers, mammals have hair or fur, and trees have leaves. Sin caused mankind to lose their glorious covering and became the only creature without a covering. Let's briefly read what happened after Adam and Eve sinned against the LORD:

> [7] Then the eyes of both of them were opened, and they knew that they were naked, and they sewed fig leaves together and made themselves coverings. [8] And they heard the sound of the LORD God walking in the garden in the cool of the day, and Adam and his wife hid from the presence of the LORD God among the trees of the garden. [9] Then the LORD God called to Adam and said to him, "Where are you?" [10] So he said, "I heard Your voice in the garden, and I was afraid because I was naked, and I hid." [11] And He said, "Who told you that you were naked? Have you eaten from the tree of which I commanded you that you should

not eat?" [21] Also for Adam and his wife the LORD God
made tunics of skin, and clothed them.

—Genesis 3:7-11, 21

Before the fall, Adam and his wife didn't wear any kind
of physical covering to cover themselves because God
Himself became their covering. After Adam and Eve
ate of the forbidden tree, their eyes were opened, and
they recognized that the glory that covered them was
no longer present with them. So, Adam and his wife
became ashamed of their nakedness and wanted to fix
the problem. They decided to sew fig leaves together to
create some sort of clothing to cover up their nakedness.
Meanwhile, when they heard the sound of God walking
in the midst of the Garden of Eden, they both hid from
His presence because they realized that the fig leaves
couldn't cover their sinful act.

Curse of the Fig Tree

Did you ever wonder why Jesus cursed the fig tree? (see
Mark 11:12-14; Matthew 21:18-22.) Some Bible scholars
view the fig tree as the tree that Jesus cursed for being
barren, representing the nation of Israel. According to
the Scriptures, the fig tree wasn't in the season to bear
fruit. So, why then did Jesus decide to curse the fig tree
that wasn't in season to bear fruit? He cursed the tree to
illustrate that mankind will no longer need fig leaves to

cover their unrighteous acts. Instead, Jesus' atonement on the cross gave His creation the right to be clothed once again with the glory of God. The cursing of the fig tree exemplified the self-righteous covering attempt that Adam and Eve made in the garden rather than turning to God for repentance. In the beginning, the enemy decided to expose Adam and Eve's nakedness, yet God decided to cover their nakedness and made an atonement, symbolizing Jesus Christ's eternal redemption. We are able to see the Father's amazing love when He decided to cover them with tunics of skins to cover their nakedness.

Noah's Nakedness

The story of Noah and his three sons is a similar illustration. Noah was drunk with wine and became naked in his tent, and one of his sons named Ham saw his father's nakedness, and instead of Ham covering his father's nakedness, he decided to tell his brothers, Shem and Japheth. Shem and Japheth didn't act like their brother Ham but immediately covered their father's nakedness (see Genesis 9:20-23). Jesus, our big bother, didn't expose our nakedness, instead He covered us with His blood, covering our nakedness.

Clean Garments

It's our responsibility as citizens of the Kingdom to keep our garments clean. In Ecclesiastes 9:8 it says, "*Let your garments always be white."* Jesus fulfilled His assignment on the cross. However, it's now our duty to keep our garments clean. The book of Exodus provides all Believers a simple instruction on how to keep our garments clean. After speaking with God on Mount Sinai, Moses arrived with good news to the nation of Israel according to the following passage from Exodus 19:10-11:

> [10] Then the Lord said to Moses, "Go to the people and consecrate them today and tomorrow, and let them wash their clothes. [11] And let them be ready for the third day. For on the third day the Lord will come down upon Mount Sinai in the sight of all the people."

In the above scriptures, God invited His people to meet with Him on Mount Sinai. But, before the people of Israel could meet with God, He gave them one prerequisite—to consecrate themselves for three days. The key to keeping our garments clean is consecrating our life to the LORD. Jesus Christ cleansed our contaminated garments with the shedding of His blood on the cross of Calvary, but it is our obligation as Christian Believers to keep our garments clean by living a consecrated life before Him. The word "consecrate" is from the Hebrew word *"qadash"* which means *to be set apart.*[4] God is calling a chosen generation to live a life set apart for Him, and to be separated from the desires and unrighteousness of the world. The apostle Paul provides us with a brief explanation on how to live a sanctified life in his second letter to the church of Corinthians:

[14] Do not be unequally yoked together with unbelievers. For what fellowship has righteousness with lawlessness? And what communion has light with darkness? [15] And what accord has Christ with Belial? Or what part has a believer with an unbeliever? [16] And what agreement has the temple of God with idols? For you are the temple of the living God. As God has said: "I will dwell in them and walk among them. I will be their God, and they shall be My people." [17] Therefore "Come out from among them and be separate, says the Lord. Do not touch what is unclean and I will receive you." [18] "I will be a Father to you, and you shall be My sons and daughters, says the Lord Almighty."

—2 Corinthians 6:14-18

Paul instructs the Corinthians to neither fellowship nor commune with the world, and to be separated from the world. The apostle refers to separating ourselves from the world as neither partaking nor practicing the unrighteousness and lawlessness of the world. God desires to receive His creation toward Him. Nevertheless, the only way He will receive His creation is if His creation will consecrate their lives to Him. He promises in the above scriptures to be our Father, and we shall be his sons or daughters if we live a life set apart toward Him.

COMMUNION

The second point in which sin contaminated the image of man was with our communion. The word "communion" simply means *fellowship, intercourse between two persons or more, mutual intercourse.*[5] The intention for God's creation wasn't only to communicate with Him, but to have intimate communion with Him. Anyone has the ability to communicate with a person. However, communion is the result of an intimate relationship. Before the fall, Adam and Eve had a relationship of intimate communion with the Creator. Therefore, sin brought a gap between man and God, separating man from His Creator.

> *God's creation wasn't only to communicate with Him, but to have intimate communion with Him.*

What Is the Consequence of Sin?

The Scripture says, *"The wages of sin is death"* (Romans 6:23a). The consequence of sin is death, and the result of death is separation. When a person dies, it brings complete separation between the family members and the deceased. The family members no longer have communion with the deceased person. In the book of Genesis, we clearly see how the sin nature separated Adam and Eve from the presence of God, and brought death:

> And they heard the sound of the Lord God walking in the garden in the cool of the day, and Adam and his wife hid themselves from the presence of the Lord God among the trees of the garden. —Genesis 3:8

Immediately after Adam and his wife ate of the forbidden tree they spiritually died, and eventually, they both died physically. Sin didn't only bring death to the human race but separated mankind from the presence of God. In the Old Testament, God provided animal sacrifices, the tabernacle, temples, and feast-days to fellowship with His people. Yet God had a perfect plan by sending His only begotten Son, Jesus Christ, to be the permanent mediator between heaven and earth, thus restoring our communion with our Creator.

Jacob and Nathanael

Jacob had a dream, and in it he saw a ladder *"set up on the earth, and its top reached to heaven; and there the angels of God were ascending and descending on it"* (Genesis 28:12). On the other hand, Nathanael had an encounter with Jesus in which He told him that he would see, *"heaven open, and the angels of God ascending and descending upon the Son of Man"* (John 1:51).

The ladder that Jacob saw in the dream symbolizes the Son of Man that was revealed to Nathanael. Jesus Christ became the bridge that reconnected heaven and earth through the redemption of His blood and crucifixion; He became the mediator between God and man (see 1 Timothy 2:5) and gave mankind full access to the Father's throne. The word "angel" used in the above scripture from Genesis 28 is the Hebrew word *"malak"* which literally means *messenger or representative.*[6] "Angel" in John 1:51 is *"Angelos"* in Greek which means *a messenger, enjoy, one who is sent, an angel, a messenger from God.*[7] If you notice in the above scriptures, the angels were first ascending to heaven, then descending to earth. Shouldn't angels first descend to earth before ascending to heaven? The angels that were revealed to Jacob and Nathanael represent a Believer of Christ bringing the kingdom of heaven to earth. You are responsible for invading the kingdom of God on earth.

Who Is Our Helper?

Jesus became our mediator, and we became Christ's ambassadors on earth to preach and to manifest the kingdom of God (2 Corinthians 5:20). Sin caused a gap between heaven and earth that prevented creation from communing with the Creator. That relationship was restored by Jesus Christ on the cross. Jesus had to ascend to heaven to fill the gap between earth and heaven. He didn't only become the bridge, but He ascended into heaven and sent us a helper. Let's see what Jesus said about the helper in the following scripture:

> Nevertheless I tell you the truth. It is to your advantage that I go away; for if I do not go away, the Helper will not come to you; but if I depart, I will send Him to you. —John 16:7

The helper that Jesus sent us is the most important person on earth—the Holy Spirit. The Holy Spirit empowers every Believer to live an extraordinary life. The leaders and Believers of the early Church in the book of Acts totally depended on, were moved by, and lived by the Holy Spirit (see Acts 5:32; 11:12,28; 13:4; 15:28; 16:6). Let's look at some of the assignations of the Holy Spirit:

The Holy Spirit empowers every Believer to live an extraordinary life.

- *He will teach you all things* (John 14:26).
- *He will bring to remembrance all things that Jesus said* (John 14:26).
- *He will bring peace* (John 14:27).
- *He will testify of Jesus* (John 15:26).

- *He will convict the world of sin, righteousness, and judgment* (John 16:8).
- *He will guide you into all truth* (John 16:13).
- *He will not speak on His own authority, but whatever He hears He will speak* (John 16:13).
- *He will tell you things to come* (John 16:13).
- *He will glorify Jesus* (John 16:14).
- *You will receive and be endued with power* (Luke 24:49, Acts 1:8).

He was the most important part of the early church. Without the Holy Spirit, there is no communion with the Heavenly Father. Jesus gives us access to the kingdom of heaven, but the Holy Spirit enables us to have communion with the Father.

AUTHORITY

Finally, the last thing that sin contaminated was man's original authority. Mankind was created to have the legal power to rule and have dominion over the earth. Let's look at what the Scriptures say in Genesis 1:26-28:

> 26 Then God said, "Let Us make man in Our image, according to Our likeness; let them have dominion over the fish of the sea, over the birds of the air, and over the cattle, over all the earth and over every creeping thing that creeps on the earth." 27 So God created man

in His own image; in the image of God He created him; male and female He created them. [28] Then God blessed them, and God said to them, "Be fruitful and multiply; fill the earth and subdue it; have dominion over the fish of the sea, over the birds of the air, and over every living thing that moves on the earth."

Adam and Eve became God's stewards of the earth and were created to rule and have dominion over every living creature on the earth.

> *Mankind was created to have the legal power to rule and have dominion over the earth.*

God always had absolute authority over the heavens and the entire universe except for the planet earth. So, why didn't God intervene when Adam and Eve ate of the forbidden tree, or why did He not stop the serpent from deceiving them? Because He gave Adam and Eve all authority on earth.

Man's Authority

Man was never created to rule over another man, but he has been given legal authority over every creation, including Satan and his demons. Any spirit without a body is an illegal alien on earth. The Creator or heavenly creatures don't intervene in the earth realm without legal permission from mankind. For instance, a demon needs a body in which to operate, or the Holy Spirit needs a vessel to manifest. Satan had to disguise himself as the serpent to deceive Eve because he had no legal right to be in the garden. On the other hand, God in bodily form came to earth as man to legally restore His throne on earth. After the fall, Adam and Eve lost all legal authority on earth, and surrendered the keys of authority to the enemy. Nevertheless, God had a plan of salvation through Jesus Christ to redeem mankind from the curse and restore creation's authority (Luke 10:19), Jesus giving man the right to be born again into the family of God (John 3:3-8).

Resurrection Power

Jesus of Nazareth defeated sin on the cross of Calvary and redeemed humanity from the sins of the world into eternal salvation. The power of the resurrection of Jesus Christ has been given to all Believers: legal authority and access into the kingdom of God, the privilege to dwell in His presence, and the opportunity to fellowship with Him. However, generations have failed because they rejected, disobeyed, and rebelled against the LORD. Nevertheless, the LORD Himself is forming a chosen generation with His own hands that will walk in the power of His glory, a generation that would neither allow the system of the world to corrupt or mold them, nor allow the enemy to deceive them. The LORD desires to manifest the fullness of His glory on earth, yet He needs an accessible vessel that will be willing to get closer to God and reflect His glory. Are you willing to become an accessible vessel in the Creator's hands? If your answer is yes, let's move on to the next chapter.

IMAGE OF MAN

The purpose of this chapter is to understand that we were created to reflect the original image of God's glory on earth.

REVIEW QUESTIONS

1. According to Genesis 1:26-27, in whose image did God create man? How do you feel knowing that you were created in His image?

   _____

   _____

   _____

2. According to the book of James 4:8, what happens when you draw near to God?

   _____

   _____

   _____

Note: It's in God's heart that you reflect His glory, however, you must draw near to Him. Drawing closer to God means to deepen your personal relationship with Him.

3. Read Isaiah 59:1-2 and write what is separating man from God.

_____

_____

_____

Note: Sin has become man's stumbling block for releasing God's glory and is what separated man from the Creator. The good news is that Jesus paid the way on the cross and demolished man's sinful nature.

PERSONAL QUESTION

1. In your own words, what does it mean to you to be created in God's image and to reflect His glory on earth?

_____

_____

_____

_____

_____

_____

CHAPTER 4

Chosen Vessel

But you are a chosen generation, a royal priesthood, a holy nation, his own special people, that you may proclaim the praises of Him who called you out of darkness into his marvelous light.

—1 Peter 2:9

I GREW UP IN BROOKLYN, New York where basketball was an influential part of my teen years. In 2005, my junior year of high school, my best-friend (Ricardo) and I decided to try out for the high school varsity basketball team. On the first day of the basketball tryouts, we started with two layup lines on each side of the basketball court. This was done to test the ability to do layups with each hand. My friend greatly lacked layup skills with his left hand, a problem which he dreaded. At first, he did well with his right. But, when he had to switch to his left hand, he did the most horrible layup I have ever seen in the game of basketball. This shocking performance gained the undivided attention of the coaches. After the tryout was done, I headed to the locker room and saw Ricardo with a disappointed and heartbroken look on his face.

I asked him, "*What happened, bro?*"

He looked back at me and said, "*I didn't make it.*"

"*For real?*"

With a sad face he responded, "*Yeah, the coach told me, 'Go home. You're not gonna make it.'*"

Confused, I said, "*What happened?*"

He said, "*It was when I tried to layup the ball with my left hand.*"

Unfortunately, my friend wasn't able to make the team roster because of this, yet out of the 40 or so students who tried out, I was one of the few selected to join the varsity basketball team. Everyone student is eligible to try out for the varsity basketball team, but not every student who shows up for tryouts is chosen. Likewise, everyone on earth is eligible to join the army of

> *God has given us a free will to choose our destiny and the right to become His chosen vessel.*

Jesus Christ, but only a few are chosen. Jesus said it this way, *"For many are called, but few are chosen"* (Matthew 22:14). Every individual on earth has a special calling from the Creator. However, not everyone who is called is chosen by default. God has given us a free will to choose our destiny and the right to become His chosen vessel.

HEART OF A CHOSEN

A person's calling doesn't guarantee that they will become a chosen vessel, but their heart condition will. As stated in a previous chapter, the Creator can see beyond what we can perceive ourselves; a man sees the outward appearance, but God sees our hearts. If we study the life of King Saul and David, we will notice that they were very similar. David and Saul were both shepherds, they were anointed by the same prophet and judge, Samuel, and they both shared similar callings from God—to become king over Israel. Despite their similarity, David became a chosen vessel of God, while Saul was rejected by God. The difference between Saul and David wasn't their calling, but their heart condition. David is known as a man after God's own heart (see Acts 13:22) because he was all about pleasing God rather than man, while Saul valued the opinion of the people rather than obeying and honoring God (see I Samuel 15:30).

David's Opportunity for the Kingship

Saul's jealousy towards David drove him to persecute David for many years. This persecution in turn drove David to the wilderness where he spent many years running for his life. In the midst of this difficult situation, David is faced with several opportunities to take Saul down, put an end to his life, and become the new king of Israel (see I Samuel 24:1-6; 26:23). But David doesn't kill Saul because he feared God, and understands the principle of honoring God's authority.

From a worldly perspective, David missed the opportunity to commence his calling as king by not killing Saul. However, David's heart was never following the fulfillment of his calling, rather, he was following God's own heart. It's sad to see people not willing to honor those in authority. Many, instead of honoring those in authority, take it upon themselves to fulfill the call of God over their lives, and are ready to kill or destroy someone else's reputation. If you deeply desire to become a chosen vessel of God, then you must seek to have a heart patterned after God's own heart.

Moses and the Promised Land

In Exodus chapter 33 we see how God offers Moses the opportunity to inherit the Promised Land, but Moses rejected God's offer. Why would Moses refuse the opportunity to possess the land that was promised by God? Perhaps it's because He understood a very important aspect of God's nature—His presence. Moses wouldn't go anywhere without the presence of God. His heart wasn't only toward reaching his destination, he wanted something more, something greater, something that God was alluding to throughout the journey with the people of Israel—His presence. God's presence is the only thing that completes and fulfills us. There is nothing wrong with following after God's promise, but sometimes we focus so much on reaching our destination, that we forget about His presence.

While writing this book, I had plenty of opportunity to rush through the process. Nevertheless, for me it wasn't only about writing a book, but also that throughout the entire process, His presence was there. What's the benefit in reaching your destination, or God's promise in your life, and knowing God isn't with you? For instance, after the Spirit of God departed from King Saul, Saul kept executing his calling as king, but God was no longer with Him, His presence had departed. The fact that you can flow in your gifts and be used by God doesn't indicate that God is with you. An example of this is when Saul started prophesying amongst the prophets, though he was flowing with the prophetic gift, he wasn't a prophet, and this was not an indicator of the permanence of God's presence upon his life. There are people like King Saul who continue in their position of God's calling, reaching after their destination, but God isn't with them. Instead of seeking the heart of God, they focus on fulfilling their calling. Instead of honoring the man of God as David honored Saul, they trample their leaders, kill them, and do anything just to execute their calling instead of aiming to become a chosen vessel of God.

Esther Versus Absalom

Esther was chosen from thousands of women to become the Queen of Persia. The question is, what distinguished Esther from the other young women that caused her to be chosen? I believe that Esther sought the king's heart while the others sought the splendor and benefits of the kingdom. The book of Esther says that:

> Each young woman went to the king, and she was given whatever she desired to take with her from the women's quarters to the king's palace. —Esther 2:13

However, when it was Esther's turn to spend the night with the king, the Scriptures say:

> Now when the turn came for Esther the daughter of Abihail the uncle of Mordecai, who had taken her as

his daughter, to go in to the king, she requested nothing but what Hegai the king's eunuch, the custodian of the women, advised. —Esther 2:15a

Every candidate had the opportunity to choose anything from the women's quarters, Esther didn't request anything, but the advice of Hegai, one of the king's eunuchs. This shows that Esther's desire was to please the king.

In the other hand, Absalom lived in Jerusalem for two years without seeing the face of David his father (see II Samuel 14:28). He had full access to the kingdom and its benefits, but he had no access to the king. God's Kingdom is the most beautiful Kingdom, but we tend to pay more attention to the beneficiary hand of the King, than to the King Himself. All the young women had access to the kingdom, but only Esther was chosen to become Queen of Persia because she desired the heart of the king.

Joshua and Caleb

Out of the millions of Israelites delivered from Egypt, do you know how many entered the Promised Land? Just two: Joshua and Caleb. They were the only men allowed to enter the Promised Land because of their heart. This is why the scripture says, *"Above all else, guard your heart, for everything you do flows from it"* (Proverbs 4:23, NIV).

Many of us focus on guarding our testimony and forget to guard our hearts, the indicator of our testimony. Now that you understand the importance of the condition of your heart, let's elaborate on three principles on how to become a chosen vessel of God.

MAKING A DECISION

Making a decision is the initial key for a chosen generation to manifest the glory of God on earth. The first step I took to join the basketball team was to simply decide to try out for the team. If we look into our daily lives, we may notice that they are filled with decisions. Some of our life decisions are insignificant, but others are extremely important. Everything a person does, from the moment they wake up in the morning, is carried out by a series of choices, such as: morning prayer, the clothes to wear, what to eat, whether to go to the gym, go to work, what book to read, what to watch on TV, and so on.

Every decision in life demands an action. For instance, if you want to lose weight, then you will have to make changes to your diet, and depending on your goal, you may be required to exercise. God didn't express His love with words alone, but He revealed His love through His actions (see John 3:16). As an act of love toward humanity, God gave His only begotten Son (Jesus Christ) to be crucified, so that we (humanity) may receive everlasting life. If you really desire to reveal God's glory, not only do you have to make a decision, but you have to act upon that decision.

Choose Your Destiny

Decisions will determine our destiny, but it may also determine the destiny of the future generations. For that reason, it's extremely important to make decisions wisely. Adam and Eve's decision to eat of the forbidden fruit set the course of their own destiny, and they were thus removed from the garden of Eden and God's presence. Furthermore, their decision affected the entire human race, causing mankind to inherit a sinful nature.

A GPS is known to help a person reach his or her destination. However, the user of the navigating

> *Decisions will determine our destiny, but it may also determine the destiny of the future generations.*

system is responsible to choose which route to take in order to reach the desired destination. For example, God gave the people of Israel their destination, which was to reach the Promised Land. Yet, it was their decision that determined their outcome. As a result of their decisions, the Israelites stayed forty years in the wilderness, when in fact, the entire journey could have taken about a few weeks. You're in charge of your own destiny, and if you desire to enter the Promised Land in your lifetime, then you have to make wise decisions.

Two Paths of Life

In the Sermon on the Mount, Jesus provides mankind with the freedom to choose their destination. Let's read what Jesus says in Matthew 7:13-14:

> [13] Enter by the narrow gate; for wide is the gate and broad is the way that leads to destruction, and there are many who go in by it. [14] Because narrow is the gate and difficult is the way which leads to life, and there are few who find it.

Jesus identifies two types of paths from which mankind must choose—the narrow path that leads to life or the broad path that leads to destruction. Then, why do most people choose the path of destruction rather than the path that leads to life? I conclude that it's because the path to life is difficult, and only few are determined to go through it. Many people try to make the right decision to enter by the narrow gate, but it's when they're faced with life's difficulties that they decide to take the easy route.

How do we successfully take the narrow way of life? The answer is found in the book of Zechariah when the LORD said to him, *"Not by might nor by power, but by My*

Spirit" (Zechariah 4:6b). For over twenty years I tried to change my life with my own strength, but I always fell short. I was addicted to pornography, alcohol, sexual lusts, and could never overcome my addictions. However, when the Holy Spirit came into my life, I understood that it was only through His empowerment that I could overcome. The Holy Spirit is the fundamental key to successfully passing through the narrow pathway.

> *The Holy Spirit is the fundamental key to successfully passing through the narrow pathway.*

Red or Blue

There is a very famous movie called *The Matrix* by the producers, Lilly and Lana Wachowski. In a scene of the movie, a character called Morpheus provides the protagonist of the movie, Neo, a decision to choose between a red or a blue pill. Let's read what Morpheus told Neo:`

> *You take the blue pill, the story ends. You wake up in your bed and believe whatever you want to believe. You take the red pill, you stay in Wonderland, and I show you how deep the rabbit hole goes.*[1]

Neo was given the choice to face reality or live his life as an illusion. What about you? Which pill are you going to take? The blue pill, which represents the wide gate, or the red pill, which represents the narrow gate? If you desire to manifest God's glory in your life, that means the narrow gate. The narrow path is the hardest journey in life, yet it is the most rewarding! Today, the choice is in your hands, so is the path of your life. If you aren't willing to follow Jesus Christ wholeheartedly, this book isn't for you. This book is written for a chosen generation who is willing to sacrifice their lives completely for Jesus Christ and follow His path. If you're willing to make that sacrifice, ask the Holy Spirit to empower you.

COUNT THE COST

When was the last time you made a wrong decision and regretted it? Or when was it that you wasted your time in an unfruitful relationship, made a wrong investment decision, or got in trouble for being in the wrong crowd? The reason for my being expelled from college, hurting the people I love, and getting myself into financial debt was due to the poor decisions I made in my life. Most of my mishaps in life are a byproduct of the poor choices I made. Nevertheless, throughout all of my mistakes, I learned the importance of counting the cost. It's rare to see people counting the cost before making a decision, because it's easier to act on impulse or emotions than to be judicious. Jesus makes this point clear in Luke 14:28-32:

> [28] For which of you, intending to build a tower, does not sit down first and count the cost, whether he has enough to finish it— [29] lest, after he has laid the foundation, and is not able to finish, all who see it begin to mock him, [30] saying, "This man began to build and was not able to finish"? [31] Or what king, going to make war against another king, does not sit down first and consider whether he is able with ten thousand to meet him who comes against him with twenty thousand? [32] Or else, while the other is still a great way off, he sends a delegation and asks conditions of peace.

Jesus provides two perfect examples here of the importance of counting the cost of a decision. As an illustration, before I decided to ask my beautiful wife, Clara to marry me, and after we got engaged, I first had to budget for the wedding and the ring, search for an apartment to move into after the wedding, find out if I had enough money to buy the furniture for the apartment, and many other things that were important in order to prepare a home for my wife and start my own family. I had to count the cost before we got married. Counting the cost means considering the consequences of an action. It's trying to figure out how such a decision can affect or benefit you and others involved. This is a very simple principle, and a necessary one, because understanding this principle and applying it, will save you from many troubles. Many are sincere in their desire to constantly make the right decision, but few are wise enough to count the cost.

PAYING A PRICE

Thousands of athletes around the world participate in a competition called the Olympic Games. The athletes that participate in the Olympics prepare themselves with months and years of hard training, sacrificing time away from their families and initiating periods of strict dieting and extreme workouts. Each athlete that participates in the Olympics pays a great price to join. Likewise, if you desire to manifest the glory of God on earth and become a true disciple of Jesus Christ, a price must be paid. Without sacrifice (or paying the price), there is no glory. Jesus Himself gave us the perfect example when He gave up His own life on the cross so that we might attain to eternal life. What makes a true disciple of Jesus Christ is one who is willing to bear his cross and come after Him—this means death to self. Many Believers desire to follow Jesus, but don't want to pay the price of discipleship, which is to take up their cross (instrument of death), and to follow Him to the place of sacrifice that brings about the glory of God. Now, let's look at what Jesus said to His disciples in Matthew 16:24-25:

> [24] If anyone desires to come after Me, let him deny himself, and take up his cross, and follow Me. [25] For whoever desires to save his life will lose it, but whoever loses his life for My sake will find it.

To follow Jesus and to surrender your life to Him means you'll be hated by the world. It's time that we

To become a chosen vessel of God, a price must be paid.

return to the narrow way and learn the cost of true discipleship in the Christian life. The Bible says in Matthew 22:14, "*For many are called, but few are chosen.*" One of the main reasons why only a few are chosen is because only a few are willing to pay the price. To become a chosen vessel of God, a price must be paid. Jesus was chosen by God to be our Messiah, yet He had to die on the cross for humanity. Joseph was chosen to rule over Egypt, but before that took place, he was sold as a slave by his brothers and was imprisoned by his master. Moses was chosen to deliver the people of Israel out of the hand of Pharaoh and lead them in the way of the Lord, but prior to that, he had to survive Pharaoh's decree. David was chosen to be king over Israel, yet he had to endure a time of persecution that came by the hand of Saul. Daniel was chosen to serve in prominent government positions after he was taken captive by the Babylonian Empire, and throughout his life he endured many trials, even surviving the lion's den. There isn't a single decision that doesn't carry with it consequences, and for every consequence, a price must be paid. If we desire to see a generation turn the world upside down for the glory of God, we must make the right decision, count the cost, and pay the price.

CHOSEN VESSEL

The purpose of this chapter was to explain the importance of having the correct heart condition in order to be a chosen vessel. We also learned the three principles on how to become a chosen vessel.

REVIEW QUESTIONS

1. What is more important to follow, God's calling or God's heart? And why?

_____

_____

_____

2. In your own words, why was David chosen and Saul rejected by God?

_____

_____

_____

3. Read Matthew 22:14 and write in your own words what this verse means.

_____

_____

_____

4. In the Sermon on the Mount, Jesus identifies two paths to life. In your own words, describe why people choose each path (Read Matthew 7:13-14).

Narrow Path:

_____

_____

_____

Broad Path:

_____

_____

_____

5. According to Luke 14:38-32, Why is counting the cost extremely important?

_____

_____

_____

6. What does Jesus tell His disciples in Matthew 16:24-25 is the consequence if they decide to deny Him?

_____

_____

_____

_____

Note: To follow Jesus means a death of self. To become a chosen vessel of God, a price must be paid, and to walk in the narrow way, we must first deny ourselves.

PERSONAL QUESTIONS

1. When was the last time you made a wrong decision and regretted it? And how did that decision affect you?

    _____

    _____

    _____

2. List three wrong decisions you have made in your life and explain what the outcome of the wrong decision was.

Decision A:

_____

_____

_____

Decision B:

_____

_____

_____

Decision C:

_____

_____

_____

3. List three right decisions you have made in your life, and explain what the outcome of the right decision was.

Decision A:

_____

_____

_____

Decision B:

_____

_____

_____

Decision C:

_____

_____

_____

4. How does counting the cost help you make a better decision?

_____

_____

_____

Personal Activity: Take a piece of paper and fold it in half. Then, on the first half of the paper, make a list of the decisions that you would like to make, or are about to make. On the second half of the paper, write a list about the consequences of those decisions. Meditate on each decision and ask yourself if you are willing to pay the price these decisions will result in.

Prayer Time: Let's take a moment and pray that God would give us wisdom to make the right decision in our life.

Heavenly Father,

The Scriptures says "If any of you lacks wisdom, let him ask of God, who gives to all liberally and without reproach, and it will be given to him" (James 1:5-6). Today, I ask you according to your Word to give me wisdom to that I could make wise decisions in my life. I also pray that You "may give to me the spirit of wisdom and revelation in the knowledge of You, that the eyes of my understanding be enlightened; that I may know what is the hope of Your calling, and what are the riches of the glory of Your inheritance, and what is the exceeding greatness of Your power toward me, according to the working of Your mighty power" (paraphrased, Ephesians 1:17-19). In the precious name of Jesus Christ I pray.

Amen

CHAPTER 5

Discovering Your Identity

When Jesus came into the region of Caesarea Philippi, He asked his disciples, saying, "Who do men say that I, the son of man, am?"

—Matthew 16:13

D ID YOU KNOW THAT out of billions of people that live on earth, you possess your own unique fingerprints, tone of voice, DNA, and eye color? God created everyone with a unique identity. So, what is identity? "Identity" *is the distinguishing character or personality of an individual.*[1] An identity is what differentiates you from everybody else. Unfortunately, thousands of people die daily without discovering their identities, meaning that people die without knowing who they are. The earth is filled with many gifted and talented people without an identity. This identity crises prevents mankind from releasing His glory.

Identity Theft

Identity theft is *the illegal use of someone else's personal information.*[2] When we hear about identity theft, a person automatically thinks

> *The greatest key to success lies in being who you are.*

of stealing personal information like a social security number or an identification card. Nonetheless, people are trying to find their identity in someone else's. For example, observe how people dress, speak, act, or try to become someone they aren't due to lack of identity. The greatest key to success lies in being who you are. It is only by being who you are that you can achieve the level of success you were destined to have. Any person that walks outside of their identity will find themselves living an unfulfilled life. Therefore, for this generation to manifest God's glory, they must learn to embrace their true self.

Double-Minded Generation

Identity crisis is a real issue this generation is facing. They struggle to identify their gender (unable to identify themselves as female or male), work a job they dislike, and live an unsatisfying life. Did you know that thousands of students in America each year pursue a career with an alarming sense of uncertainty? The following are some college statistics found in a quick Google search:

- *57% of students enrolled in college are not done after six years. Of that 57%, 33% of them drop out entirely. The remaining 24% stay enrolled in school, either full- or part-time.* [3]

- *28% of students drop out before completing their 2nd year.* [3]

- *27% of grad students get employed in major-related careers.* [4]

- *An estimated 20 to 50 % of students enter college as undecided, and an estimated 75 % of students change their major at least once before graduation.* [5]

These statistics illustrate that more than 50% of college students pursue a career with an uncertain mindset, 28% of students drop out of school without getting a degree, and about 73% of the students who graduate are not employed in their choice career field. It's painful to see those statics. How confused our generation is about who they are! Not knowing what God created you to be will result in living a confused, frustrated life. Only our Creator knows our identity, and if we don't have a relationship with our Creator, then we will never know who we are and will live an unfilled life.

The Apostle James states in his letter that "a *double-minded man is unstable in all his ways*" (James 1:8 KJV). A double-minded man is a person that is unsure, doubtful, and confused, reflecting an unstable lifestyle. The reason this generation is changing majors or drop-ping out of college and living an unstable lifestyle

If we don't have a relationship with our Creator, then we will never know who we are.

is because they can't discover who they are. Not only does the world not know who they are, but the Church doesn't know who they are either. Dr. Lance Wallnau stated that 80% of the body of Christ never makes it into the work that God called them to do.[6] This means that 8 out of 10 Believers don't know who they are in Christ.

Life Experience

I was one of many students who was double minded in my ways. So, I know how it feels to pursue a career with uncertainty for the sake of obtaining a degree. From a young age, my parents told me that to be successful in life, I was required to go to school and get a college degree. Nevertheless, real success does not depend on a career but on what God calls you to be. Out of all my college friends that graduated, the majority of them are not working in their career fields. They struggle to find jobs and the jobs they have they dislike.

Real Life Success

The education system has taught our generation a false reality of success. A successful life is defined by our education

> *Success isn't determined by the level of education or the degree a person may obtain, it's determined by the Creator's purpose for their life.*

system as an occupation that will provide a good paycheck. The concept that an individual's degree determines their level of success is unrealistic. Many successful people in the world never went to high school, and many dropped out of college. Some people that are examples of this are as follows: Steve Jobs, Apple CEO; Bill Gates, Microsoft CEO, comedian Steve Harvey, and so forth. Success isn't determined by the level of education or the degree a person may obtain, it's determined by the Creator's purpose for their life. True success comes when a person walks in alignment with the purpose of God in his or her life. Let me make myself clear, I'm not encouraging anyone to drop out of college or to not proceed with an education career. Personally, I'm always educating myself, however, I want to challenge every reader to search out why you're here on earth. If it's to become a doctor, teacher, engineer, minister, entrepreneur, whatever it is, then pursue it with all your heart. It's so essential to know who you are because a person without an identity is as a mute person asking a blind person for direction.

Fake Society

The world has become what I call a fake society, meaning that the world is filled with people that aren't authentic. For instance, there are teachers in the education system that aren't called to be teachers, or doctors in the hospital field that aren't meant to be doctors, or pastors in the church that were never called to become a shepherd. The lack of identity is affecting the entire human race and is preventing generations from releasing God's glory on the earth. We must understand that body of Christ is made with different members, and each member has a specific purpose (see 1 Corinthians 12:12-27). For example, the hand is created to grab, the feet to walk, and the tongue to taste food. Each body part has a function in the body, and each person has a function in the body of Christ. For some, their part is to build a business, work in the government, be ministers of the gospel, and so on. However, the problem is that people tend to try to become a part of the body that they aren't meant to be. Imagine trying to walk with your face, run with your hands, or eat with your feet. That's exactly what people in our society are doing, trying to become someone they're not. My goal in this chapter is to help you discover your identity as I discuss the following areas by which an individual's personality is defined: gifting, purpose, clothing, and vocabulary.

GIFTING

If you could have any type of superpower, what would it be? Would it be super speed, invisibility, super strength, mind-control, flying, or another choice? Growing up, many of us wanted to have a superpower. I remember when I was a child, I would play superheroes versus villains with my friends. We would pretend to be our favorite superhero or villain character and would fight each other. Both superheroes and villains have

> *A gift without God becomes corrupted.*

supernatural abilities. The villain uses his power for evil, and the superhero uses his power for good. Every person has a special supernatural gift within them. However, the way a person uses his or her gifting could determine whether they become a superhero or a villain. For example, Adolf Hitler had a strong gift of leadership. Hitler was able to communicate well and influence an entire nation. But he used his gifting to bring destruction. In my college years, I was trying to write a worldly book on how to pick-up girls. I was using my gift to influence other students on the wrong path. A gift without God becomes corrupted. If you want to see your gift flourish, place it in God's hands. Let's look at some examples in the following Scriptures:

- *Bezalel was gifted by God to design artistic works* (Exodus 31:1-5).
- *Daniel was gifted to understand visions and dreams* (Daniel 1:17).
- *Daniel and his three friends were gifted by God with knowledge and wisdom, and they were found to be ten times better than all magicians or astrologers in Babylon* (Daniel 1:17,20).
- *Salvation is a free gift given to man by God* (John 3:16).

What Is a Gift?

One of the keys to identifying who you are is to identify your gift. The word "gift" in Greek is *charisma*, which means *a favour with which one receives without any merit of his own.*[7] In the Merriam Webster Dictionary means *something voluntarily transferred by one person to another without compensation.*[8] Therefore, a gift is something that isn't earned. Yet, a gift is a free inheritance that an individual receives from another individual.

Our Creator has deposited an irrevocable gift within each of us (see Romans 11:29). It cannot be stolen or taken away, but instead, it can become dormant or manipulated by the enemy. Let's read what the book of Proverbs, said concerning our gifts, *"A man's gift makes room for him, and brings him before great men"* (Proverbs 18:16). King Solomon,

> *Your gift will enable you to fulfill your vision and your life's purpose.*

understood the importance of being able to identify your gifting. It's a person's gift that opens the door to success. Your gift will enable you to fulfill your vision and your life's purpose. When you exercise your gift, it will create a pathway to your destination.

Gifts Versus Skills

First, a person must be able to differentiate between gifts and skills. A *gift* is a free inheritance from our Creator, while a *skill* is a learned ability turned into action. I enjoy the game of basketball, and I consider myself a decent, mid-range shooter. Yet, I wasn't born with my shooting skills; they were rather, developed with time. One of the issues in determining one's gift is that people confuse their skills and passions with their gifts. If a person can cook, it doesn't automatically mean that the person was born to become a chef, or if a person loves animals, it doesn't mean they are called to become a veterinarian.

Do not confuse your passions or your skills with your gift. It can be deceitful and block you from reaching your true potential.

As I stated in the book of Proverbs that it is our gift, not our education, that makes room for us and brings us before great men. I'm not against education, rather, I believe that education should be used to develop your gift. At school, a student learns to read, write, communicate, solve math problems, and many other skills which are very important in life. Meanwhile, the education system focuses on developing your skills, not your gifts. That's why we see students dropping out of school, employees hating their jobs, and individuals living unsatisfying lives. Many people are deceived into believing that the skills they have learned in their lives will bring them to what the world defines as "true success." Some people define success by having their dream car, their dream home, an ideal family, or obtaining financial freedom. Nevertheless, the life they are living leaves them miserable inside. True success comes when you first give your life to Jesus Christ and begin to operate in your earthly assignment.

What Is Your Gift?

Perhaps you are asking yourself, "What is my gift?" It's something that comes naturally and doesn't require a lot of effort to perform. Some examples of people's gifts are as follows: making people laugh, communicating, solving problems, serving, storytelling, counseling, teaching, helping others, and more. One of my gifts is leadership. From a young age, I was always the leader of the group, and I've had the privilege of being an influencer. It's not something I've longed or searched for; it's something that happens naturally. Remember, your gift is a free inheritance that you were born with, and it needs to be discovered by you. If you don't know your gift, ask God, your Creator. He knows exactly what your gifting is and the purpose of your gift. The Bible says, *"Ask, and it will be given to you"* (Matthew 7:7a). If you don't ask, don't expect to receive it. Before you continue reading, take a few minutes and pray to the Father to help you discover your gift.

Joseph the Dreamer

Let's look at the story of Joseph and see how his gift made room for him and placed him before great men (see Genesis 37-47). Joseph was born with the gift of dreaming. Dreaming was Joseph's gift; he didn't pray for or ask God to impart the gift of dreaming to him. At the age of seventeen, Joseph had a dream and told it to his brothers, which got him into great trouble. Joseph's gifting to dream caused his brothers to hate him and sell him as a slave. He ended up in Egypt working for Potiphar, an officer of Pharaoh and captain of the guard. The LORD was with Joseph, and Potiphar made him overseer of his house. When Potiphar's wife tried to lay with Joseph, he ran away from her and then he was accused of trying to lie with her. Potiphar got angry and sent Joseph to prison. In prison, Joseph had the opportunity to interpret two dreams. After a period of time, Pharaoh had a dream and Joseph was the only one that could interpret the dream. The story ends with Joseph being placed in a position of authority at the right hand of Pharaoh.

Joseph's gift drew him to the worst moment in his life; meaning that the hardship brought his best season in his life. It may seem that things are going wrong in your life; yet the LORD is preparing you to bring you before great men. When we began reading the story of Joseph, we read about a young boy with the ability to dream, but after the process of God preparing Joseph's gifting, he was not only a dreamer, but he also possessed the ability to interpret dreams.

In this story, we clearly see how Joseph's gift made room for his destination and placed him at the right hand of Pharaoh. Your gift may cause your peers to feel uncomfortable; they may end up criticizing, hating, or even envying you. Your gift will drive you into difficulties in life. The Scripture says that "*God is a consuming fire*" (Hebrew 12:29), and if you desire to see the glory of God released in your life, you must pass through the fire. Fire is used to purify gold. Gold is a precious metal that many people use to adorn themselves, but before gold becomes valuable, it must be refined by fire. God is the potter, and He is forming in us a glorious vessel. However, the vessel must pass through the kiln's fire to become usable. There is no glory without being refined by fire. If you desire your gift to function at its maximum capacity, it must be refined by the Potter's hand.

Daniel

Another great example of finding your gift is the story of Daniel. Daniel was taken captive by Babylon, where He served under King Nebuchadnezzar. Daniel had the gift of understanding visions and dreams. His gifting enabled him to know the king's dream and interpret it. Daniel's gift promoted him to become the ruler over the whole province of Babylon (see Daniel 2:48).

Exercise Your Gift

When you identify your gift, then it's time to develop and exercise new skills. Let's say that your gift is serving and you decide to work as a server in a restaurant. Every customer you attend is extremely pleased with your service. After a few years of working in the restaurant, you decide to learn a different skill to further develop your gift, so you decide to study leadership, business, management, and accounting. Then you decide to open your own restaurant to bring the best service possible to a community. Your gift is given to you by God to be developed and to bless others.

The Parable of the Talents

The perfect example of developing your gift is the parable of the talents. In Matthew 25:14-30, Jesus spoke about the parable of the talents in which a man left his house to travel and entrusted his goods to his three servants. The first servant received five talents, the second received two, and the last received only one. After a period of time, the man came back from his long journey to get the accounts from his three servants. The first two servants doubled the value of their talents while the last servant buried his talent in the ground. The man gratefully rewarded both servants who doubled his profits, but the last servant who decided to bury his talent was punished.

The master represents the LORD, and the talents represent our gifts which God has placed in us. The moral of the parable is to be fruitful with what the LORD has trusted you. We're responsible for being fruitful with God's gift in our lives. Ask yourself what you are doing with the gifts that God has deposited in your life. (*Spend a few minutes to meditate and reflect on the question.*) Remember, inside of you is a special gift designed to impact thousands of people, but it's waiting to be awakened, used, and developed. Therefore, I encourage you to stir up the gift of God that is in you (see 2 Timothy 1:6).

PURPOSE

The second area to discuss when discovering your identity is your purpose. Rick Warren's book, "*The Purpose Driven Life,*" has sold over 30 million copies. The question, "Why are we here on earth?" is a simple question that over 30 million people can't answer. "Why I am here on earth?" was the hardest question I had to answer in my life. If you desire to know why you're here, simply ask God, the One Who knows all things and created you. Our Creator is the only One who knows exactly the purpose for which you were created.

Myles Munroe made one of the most powerful statements that impacted my entire life. He said, "*The greatest tragedy in life is not death, but a life without purpose.*"9 Dying without fulfilling your life's purpose is like living a life as though you were never born. A person is truly born when they can know why they are here on earth. It isn't until a person can answer that question that they can begin living.

After you know why you're here on earth, then your gift will help you execute God's purpose in your life. Let's say that when you turned eighteen, your parents decided to buy you a brand-new car as a birthday gift, but they decided not to give you the car key. You have this beautiful, brand-

> *It's God's duty to hide His purpose within man, but it's our mission to search out and discover it.*

new car in the garage that you're unable to use because you don't have hold of the key. The key is symbolic of your purpose and the car of your gift. And until you get hold of the key, you'll never fully operate in your gift, which is the car. The purpose of your gift is to help you execute God's blueprint in your life. So, you may ask yourself, "How am I able to find my life purpose?" The purpose that you are searching for is already in you. It's God's duty to hide His purpose within man, but it's our mission to search out and discover it.

Purpose Versus Assignment

First, we must understand the difference between a purpose and an assignment. Both purpose and assignment correlate with each other but have a slight difference. A *purpose* is simply why you are here on earth, and an *assignment* is *a* specific and designated responsibility on earth. In the Scriptures, we notice that every man or woman of faith had their own unique assignment. God has a special assignment in heaven for you ready to be released on earth. Let's look at some examples in the Scriptures.

Adam

Since the days of Adam until now, every person on earth was born with a specific assignment. One of Adam's assignments was to name every animal on earth. How did Adam have the capability of naming millions of animals and remembering each one of them? Adam's special assignment enabled him to perform the supernatural. And your assignment is going to release the supernatural ability of God in your life.

Prophets

Every prophet recorded in the Bible had the same purpose: to be God's mouthpiece. But all of the prophets had different assignments. Let's look at a few examples:

- *John the Baptist's message was the baptism of the remission of sin, and repentance toward God.*

- *Jeremiah was known as the weeping prophet, who warned the people of Israel to repent and foretold of the exile of Babylon and of the fall of Jerusalem.*

- *Daniel was a prophet in exile who spoke about the rise and fall of empires and of the end of times.*

Twelve Apostles

All twelve apostles were called for the Great Commission (Matthew 28:16-20), yet all of them possessed a special assignment. For example, the apostle Paul was specifically called to preach to the Gentiles. Paul had the grace given by God to minister to the Gentiles.

Importance of an Assignment

It is important for a person to identify their life assignment because it will bring direction in their walk with God. A purpose in a person's life will bring clarity to his or her life. Meanwhile, an assignment provides you with a specific direction. In other words, a man without an assignment is a man without direction.

Blood on Your Hands

A Believer who doesn't accomplish their purpose will face consequences and must give an account to the LORD. Let's look at what the LORD told Ezekiel:

> [7] So you, son of man: I have made you a watchman for the house of Israel; therefore you shall hear a word from My mouth and warn them for Me. [8] When I say to the wicked, 'O wicked man, you shall surely die!' and you do not speak to warn the wicked from his way, that wicked man shall die in his iniquity; but his blood I will require at your hand. [9] Nevertheless if you warn

the wicked to turn from his way, and he does not turn from his way, he shall die in his iniquity; but you have delivered your soul. – Ezekiel 33:7-9

Ezekiel was recognized as one of the Major Prophets in the Bible. In the scripture above,

A man without an assignment is a man without direction.

we're able to see that the LORD gave Ezekiel a specific purpose as a watchman for the house of Israel. However, God warned Ezekiel of the consequence of not fulfilling it. The LORD told Ezekiel that if he didn't carry out his purpose, then the blood of the people of Israel would be upon him.

In a similar manner, if you don't carry out your purpose, then the blood of those who He has given you will be upon you. Jesus Himself was responsible for the disciples given to Him by the Father (read John 17:6-8). I'm not trying to place fear in your life, but I want you to understand the importance of carrying out your purpose and assignment in your life.

A person isn't judged by his work, yet a person will be judged by what he was called to do and whether or not he completes it. God isn't impressed by how many demons a person casts out or how many miracles, signs, and wonders a person performs; neither is He impressed by how many accurate prophecies a person spoke. An individual will be judged by what God called them to do. Remember, the purpose that God placed in His creation wasn't given to be buried, it was given to man to be carried out and to eventually release His glory.

CLOTHING

The third area of discovering your identity is through your clothing. Clothing plays an important role in our identity. For example, how can a person recognize a police officer, a chef, or a doctor? Simply by the clothes they wear. A person's attire speaks a lot about his or her identity. An individual without an identity has the tendency to clothe themselves as someone else. I'm not referring to physical clothing but to putting on someone else's personality. We see this everywhere when people try to become like or act as their favorite celebrity.

What Defines Your Clothing?

The way a person clothes themselves is defined by what voice they hear. For example, a person who listens to rock music tends to dress up as a rocker, or a person who listens to rap music dresses up as a rapper. What do your clothes say about you?

Jacob and Esau

Let's look at the story of Jacob and Esau and what made

Jacob clothe himself as his older brother Esau to steal his blessing. Let's read Genesis 27:6-8; 15-16:

> [6] So Rebekah spoke to Jacob her son, saying, "Indeed I heard your father speak to Esau your brother, saying, [7] 'Bring me game and make savory food for me, that I may eat it and bless you in the presence of the LORD before my death.' Now therefore, my son, obey my voice according to what I command you." [15] Then Rebekah took the most precious clothes of Esau, her eldest son, which she had at home, and dressed Jacob, her youngest son. [16] And he put the skins of the goats on his hands and on his neck, where he had no hair.

Jacob listened to his mother and clothed himself as his elder brother, Esau. This enabled him to deceive his father Isaac to receive the blessing. Jacob stole his brother's identity to be blessed. Oftentimes, people rob themselves of their blessings by trying to become someone else. Not knowing who you are can be extremely dangerous because any voice has the potential to influence you.

Radio Frequency

In the world, there are thousands of radio stations operating at the same time. If a person desires to hear a specific radio station, they must tune into the right frequency. In life, tuning your ears to the wrong frequency may deviate you from God's purpose or destroy your life. Let's look at some examples of people who tuned into the wrong frequency:

- *Why did Adam and Eve sin against God? Both Adam and Eve heeded the wrong frequency.*

- *In Job's trials, many voices wanted to confuse him. Yet, Job never let those voices define him.*

- *The army of Israel feared the giant Goliath, but David knew the God of Israel and refused to let other voices intimidate him.*

- *Elijah was in the cave after he ran from Jezebel. A wind, an earthquake, and a fire passed and the LORD was not there. Then came a still small voice, and the LORD was there. Elijah learned to tune into the correct frequency to hear God's voice.*

We must learn to tune into God's frequency. There will be many voices we could listen to in our lives, but the only voice that matters is the voice of God. The voice that defines a man or woman of God is the voice of God. Take heed to the voice of God in your life and let that be the voice that defines you. If the LORD said that you are going to be a businessman, a doctor, a preacher, a teacher, or other, start dressing and walking like one.

VOCABULARY

Finally, your vocabulary must be aligned with your purpose. For example, If God calls you to be the next Smith Wigglesworth or a future president of the United States of America, but you spend your whole life saying, "*I can't, or I'm not qualified,*" what do you think will happen? Nothing is going to happen until you begin to call things that don't exist as though they do exist (see Romans 4:17).

After I gave my life to Jesus Christ in 2012, I told my brothers and sisters in Christ that I would get married in 2017, and some of them laughed at me. My mom thought I was crazy because I always kept reminding her of the year I was going to get married.

My mom would always say to me, "*You don't even have a girlfriend and you're thinking about marriage!*"

Then when I began dating and she became my girlfriend, my mother would say, "*You don't have a job.*"

When I found a job, she would say, "*You're just joking.*"

After I bought the engagement ring, I told my mom that I was going to get engaged, and she said, "*So you are very serious about it.*"

I got married on March 11, 2017. With the words from your own mouth, you have the power to speak into existence what the LORD said about you. If you desire to see God's promises come to fulfillment in your life, change your vocabulary. In your vocabulary, there can't be any excuse; there has to be faith. Faith is a key element in the success of your life. You may not see God's promises in your life now, but you must keep believing and speaking in faith until you see your dream turn into reality.

Jesus Knew His Identity

Jesus knew who He was. He didn't let society define Him. He asked His disciples in Matthew 16:13, "*Who do men say that I, the Son of Man, am?*"

The disciples weren't sure who Jesus was, so they started naming powerful men of God. They said, "*Some say John the Baptist, some Elijah, and others Jeremiah or one of the prophets*" (Matthew 16:14).

Then He asked them to forget who people say that He is. In verse 15 He said, "*But who do you say that I am?*"

Jesus Christ didn't allow other voices to define Who He was because He was a man with an identity. People will try to define you or compare you to someone, but what makes you unique is yourself. Every prophet recorded in the Bible had the same purpose; to be God's mouthpiece, but all of them had different assignments. You are a special and unique piece of the body of Christ. Don't let anyone in the world define who you are, except God.

DISCOVERING YOUR IDENTITY

The purpose of this chapter is to help you discover your identity by learning to embrace and discover your true self in order to manifest God's glory.

REVIEW QUESTIONS

1. According the Merriam Webster dictionary, what is identity?

   _____

   _____

2. Read James 1:8, and write in your own words, why a double man is unstable.

   _____

   _____

3. What does Paul say in Romans 11:29 concerning our gifts?

   _____

   _____

4. What did Paul tell Timothy concerning his gift? (Read 2 Timothy 1:6.)

   _____

   _____

5. Can you give some examples in the Scriptures of God's people using their gift?

    _____

    _____

6. What made Jacob disguise himself as his older brother Esau? (Read Genesis 27:6-8; 15-16.)

    _____

    _____

Note: Not knowing who you are can be extremely dangerous because any voice has the potential to influence you. Jesus Christ didn't allow other voices to define Who He was because He was a man with an identity. Jesus knew Who He was. He didn't let society define Him.

PERSONAL QUESTIONS

1. What do people say about you compared to what God says about you?

    _____

    _____

2. If you could have any type of superpower, what would it be and why?

    _____

    _____

3. Can you name one of your gifts, and what can you
    do to develop it?

    _____

    _____

4. What voices are speaking upon your life, and do
    those voices align with what God said about you?

    _____

    _____

Reflection Activity: Please, take moment to answer the
questions in the back of this book that will help you
to know about your true self (**See Appendix I**).

Prayer Time: Let's take a moment and pray that God
will help us discover our gift and purpose in our life.
(Read Jeremiah 29:11)

Heavenly Father,

*I personally thank You that You have plans to prosper
me, and plan to give me a future and a hope. I pray
that You reveal to me the gift You've given me, and help
me to discover the purpose that You have for my life
that I may reveal Your glory on earth. In the precious
name of Jesus Christ I pray.*

Amen

CHAPTER 6

Walking In Your Identity

I, therefore, the prisoner of the LORD, beseech you to walk worthy of the calling with which you were called.

—Ephesians 4:1

WE NEED TO LEARN how to walk in our identities as well as knowing our identity. Paul wrote to the Ephesian church, "*I, therefore, the prisoner of the LORD, beseech you to walk worthy of the calling with which you were called*" (Ephesians 4:1). Paul emphasizes the importance of walking in our purpose. In the previous chapter, we learned how to discover our identity. In this chapter, I'll be discussing three essential keys to walking in your identity.

OBEDIENCE

Obedience is the first key to successfully walking in your identity. If you want to effectively walk in your identity, you must obey God's commands in your life. Here is what the prophet Samuel had to say about obedience in 1 Samuel 15:22:

> Has the LORD as great delight in burnt offerings and sacrifices, as in obeying the voice of the LORD? Behold, to obey is better than sacrifice.

Samuel explained it clearly. A person's obedience toward God is better than any type of sacrifice. Disobedi-

Obedience is an essential key if you desire to see the glory of God manifest in your life.

ence is the number one issue mankind has struggled with from the beginning of creation. The judgment that Israel received wasn't for lack of offerings, or sacrifices, but rather for their disobedience. If the LORD was searching for obedience when He created mankind, what do you think He's still searching for? Our obedience! Obedience is an essential key if you desire to see the glory of God manifest in your life.

Importance of Obedience

Throughout my walk with Christ, I have learned the power of obedience. Obedience is the most important key to life's success. Prayer, fasting, the Word of God, and worship, are considered the four most essential tools for a Believer. However, what makes these four tools effective in a person's life is obedience. It isn't how much you pray, fast, read the Word, or worship God. It's about your obedience to God. How many times does the Holy Spirit wake us up in the middle of the night to pray, or urge us to read the Bible during the day, or lead us to fast, and we ignore Him? The Lord's anointing in a person's life is released through obedience. If you desire to see a greater release of God's anointing, begin to obey. Remember, if you're faithful to obey in the little things God desires, then the LORD can trust you with greater things in His kingdom.

Noah's Ark

The story of the ark of Noah is one of the most famous stories in the book of Genesis (see Genesis 6-8). The wickedness of man was so great on earth that the LORD decided to destroy the earth with a flood. *"But Noah found grace in the eyes of the LORD"* (Genesis 6:8), and He decided to spare Noah and his family by building an ark. First, we must understand that Noah had never seen an ark in his lifetime, and the LORD commanded Noah to build something that had never been built before. Second, Noah is building an ark because it is going to rain. Mankind had never seen rain until the flood came. How would you react if you were in Noah's position? Would you say, "God, are joking with me?" Or when the ark was being built, do you think people said things like, "Noah must be going crazy! He has some type of mental problem"? Or maybe people were making fun of him. The good news is that Noah built the ark and saved his family because of his obedience.

Build Your Own Ark

God is calling you to build your own ark. Not a physical ark like Noah's, but an ark of dreams or visions that may seem unrealistic to you. Obedience toward God doesn't mean to obey Him when it seems good to you, but to obey Him regardless of if it seems logical. The promises that God spoke over your life can seem impossible and those around you may laugh about it or discourage you. Remember, with man, it is impossible, but with God, all things become possible (Matthew 19:26). Let's look at some examples:

- *The walls of Jericho fell after the Israelites marched around the city 13 times in a span of seven days* (Joshua 6:1-27).

- *Peter was asked by Jesus to go fishing in the lake and take a coin out of the first fish he caught to pay their taxes* (Matthew 17:24-27).

- *Nehemiah was rebuilding the walls of Jerusalem, and the enemy was laughing and mocking the Jews when they heard what he was about to do* (Nehemiah 4:1).

An act of your obedience toward the calling of God in your life can bring an impact or change around the world. He is just waiting for you to obey.

Simon Peter

Peter was a fisherman by occupation, so I imagine that he knew a lot about fishing—the best time, locations, and even the best seasons to fish. Nevertheless, in his encounter with the LORD, we learn that Peter had a horrible day at fishing—he wasn't able to catch anything! I imagine how tired and frustrated Peter must've felt after such an unfruitful day of work. It was at this moment of failure, having caught nothing through the whole night and day, that Jesus appeared and told Peter to cast the net down. When Peter cast the net down, he had a miraculous catch. The catch was so big that the net began to break (see Luke 5).

Obedience was the key to Peter's miraculous catch of fish. The instant Peter obeyed Jesus' command was the instant a miracle manifested in his life. A miracle awaits you, but it requires your obedience. At times Believers don't live an extraordinary life for lack of obedience. They tend to shout and rejoice at God's Word but don't do anything with the word that God spoke over their life. Discovering who you are is the first step, yet the next important step is to obey and begin to walk in the calling of God in your life.

FAITH

The second key to walking in your identity is having faith. If you want to walk in your identity, you must live a life of faith. David Yonggi Cho said, *"God will never bring about any of His great works without coming through your own personal faith."*[1] Faith is the key that will help you accomplish your earthly assignment. Let's look at the following examples of faith:

- *By faith Abel offered to God a more excellent sacrifice than Cain, through which he obtained witness that he was righteous, God testifying of his gifts; and through it he being dead still speaks* (Hebrews 11:4).

- *By faith Enoch was taken away so that he did not see death, "and was not found, because God had taken him"; for before he was taken he had this testimony, that he pleased God* (Hebrews 11:5).

- *By faith Noah, being divinely warned of things not yet seen, moved with Godly fear, prepared an ark for the saving of his household, by which he condemned the world and became heir of the righteousness which is according to faith* (Hebrews 11:7).

- *By faith Abraham obeyed when he was called to go out to the place which he would receive as an inheritance. And he went out, not knowing where he was going* (Hebrews 11:8).

What Is Faith?

So, what is faith? *"Faith is the substance of things hoped for, the evidence of things not seen"* (Hebrews 11:1). I define faith with two simple words: *belief* and *hope*. For example, I was hoping and believing in God that I would get married in 2017, and I did. God has an amazing plan for your life, yet we're only able to see a glimpse of our future. Therefore, it takes faith to believe and hope in God that it will eventually come to pass. I took a leap of faith writing this book. There was a time I wanted to quit and give up. Nevertheless, I kept believing and hoping in the words the LORD had spoken over my life. God will test our faith to see if we really trust in Him.

Why Faith Is Important?

Do you know what the Bible says about faith? *"But without faith it is impossible to please Him"* (Hebrews 11:6a). The author of the book of Hebrews clarifies that without faith, no one can please God. If you deeply desire to please God, then you must live a life of faith.

How Does Faith Come?

Then, how does faith come to the Believer? Romans 10:17 says, *"So then faith comes by hearing, and hearing by the word of God."* The Word of God is the spiritual food that every Christian Believer needs. A person's spiritual nutrition depends totally on the Word of God. Jesus Himself said in the Gospels that *"man shall not live by bread alone, but by every word that proceeds from the mouth of God"* (Matthew 4:4b). Why do you think Noah had faith to build an ark or Abraham had faith to go out to an unknown place? It is because they both received faith when they heard God's voice in their life.

How Do You Build Your Faith?

When you feel weak and that you want to give up, begin to listen to those words that the LORD has spoken over your life, and repeat them over and over again until those words produce faith.

Another way to build up your faith is found in the book of Jude, which says, *"But you, beloved, building yourselves up on your most holy faith, praying in the Holy Spirit"* (Jude 1:20). Speaking in tongues is a powerful tool you can use to build up your faith.

What Is the Enemy of Faith?

The enemy will try to do everything he can to destroy your faith. The enemy of faith is fear. When fear comes into a Christian's life, it means that the faith of the Believer is deactivated. The enemy knows that if he can bring fear into your life, then he can defuse your faith. So, how do you defeat fear? 1 John 4:18 says, *"There is no fear in love; perfect love casts out fear."* For instance, one night my two-year-old son woke up in the middle of the night crying. But, when he saw me draw closer to him and heard my voice, he felt secure and safe. Why? Because the effect of true love casts all fear. God is love, and it is His love that helps us overcome our fears.

Walk By Faith

If you desire to see God's promises accomplished in your life, you must walk by faith, and not by what you see in the natural realm. The LORD told the people of Israel to march thirteen times around the walls of Jericho to destroy it (see Joshua 6). In the natural eyes, God's commands seem absurd, and many of our promises may seem insane. Yet, it doesn't matter how illogical God's command may seem to you; all you have to do is walk by faith, believing, and hoping in God. There are going to be walls in your life that will try to prevent you from conquering your Promised Land. Remember, walk by faith, believing in God with all your heart, and you will see those walls begin to fall.

TRUST

The last key to walking in your identity is trust. Trust means assurance, reliance, and having confidence in another person. God is calling you to trust your life wholeheartedly to Him. The Bible says in Proverbs 3:5-6:

> 5 Trust in the LORD with all your heart, and lean not on your own understanding; 6 In all your ways acknowledge Him, and He shall direct your paths.

Our steps are directed by the LORD when we learn to put our trust in Him.

Supernatural

Trusting in God means believing in the supernatural. God's power goes beyond science, a doctor's diagnosis, or any situation. God has the power to heal all types of sicknesses and diseases (especially, in the area where doctors don't have an answer), to create miracles, to deliver you from death, depression, and addiction, or deliver you from any type of demonic activity in your life.

God has the power to change what seems impossible into reality. Remember, His ways are higher than man, and if we desire to see the supernatural power of God operate in our lives, we must begin to trust in Him, and not in our own abilities or understanding.

Surrender

To trust God means to surrender your entire life to Him. For example, in the book of Genesis, God told Abraham to go to the mountain and sacrifice his son Isaac. After 25 years of waiting for the promise of his son, God instructed Abraham to sacrifice his beloved son. As a father, I can only imagine how difficult that decision was for Abraham. Abraham had to trust God with all His heart, and that is what God is waiting for us to do—totally surrender our lives to Him. Trusting God means trusting Him with everything that is precious to us, such as: wife, children, ministry, material possessions. We ought to be like the woman who poured out the alabaster jar upon Jesus that cost her almost a year's worth of wages. In other words, God demands that we, His children, completely surrender to Him that which is most precious to us. To trust means that we must detach ourselves completely from the world and abide with Him. Trusting in the LORD will require that we give Him our most precious and important things.

Walking In Your Identity

Obedience, faith, and trust are necessary if you desire to reach your destination. I have seen many Believers receive prophetic words from God and stay stagnant their entire life, waiting for that word to come to pass. So, why doesn't the word come to pass? Because they don't take a leap of faith, an act of obedience to God. The prophetic word also doesn't come to pass because they don't trust the LORD wholeheartedly.

God spoke to me and told me to write. I had the choice to obey or ignore it. I didn't know how to begin, but I trusted in God and took a leap of faith. If you don't work on your earthly assignment, the LORD will raise someone else to perform your responsibility. For example, Saul was anointed king over Israel. However, God raised David as his successor because Saul wasn't able to fulfill his assignment. God has an amazing plan for your life, but if you aren't willing to obey, walk by faith, and trust Him, He will raise someone else to fill your assignment. I want to encourage you to follow your dream, vision, and purpose in life, and begin to walk in them before it's too late. Remember, tomorrow isn't promised, but today is (see Proverbs 27:1; Matthew 6:34). Don't wait for tomorrow, next week, next month, or next year. Start taking action today. Take one step at a time until you reach your destination.

WALKING IN YOUR IDENTITY

The purpose of this chapter is to learn three essentials to walking in our identities.

REVIEW QUESTIONS

1. According to 1 Samuel 15:22, what does the LORD delight in the most?

   _____

2. Read Hebrews 11:1 and write in your own words what faith is and how faith will help you walk in your own identity.

   _____

   _____

3. According to the book of Proverbs 3:5-6, what is the key to our steps being directed by the LORD?

   _____

   _____

PERSONAL QUESTIONS

1. Do you have issues or difficulties obeying God's call in your life? If yes, why?

   _____

   _____

2. What do you fear most in your life, and has fear prevented you from walking in your calling? If yes, how?

_____

_____

_____

3. Can you identify your Isaac in your life, and are you willing to sacrifice it to the Lord?

_____

_____

_____

Prayer Time: Let's take a moment and pray that God will help us surrender our Isaac on the altar of God. (Read Genesis 22:2.)

Heavenly Father,

Today, I want to surrender my Isaac ,_____
(Put a name to your Isaac). *Father, anything in life that is first place rather than You, today I surrender it to You because I understand that I can't do anything without You. Help me to be the best version of You in the earth, that I may glorify and exalt your name. In the precious name of Jesus Christ I pray.*

Amen

CHAPTER 7

Treasure Hunt

It is the glory of God to conceal a matter, but
the glory of kings is to search out a matter.
—Proverbs 25:2

CLARA AND I HAD been courting for a while and by
the summer of 2016, it was time to pop the question—would she marry me? Therefore, I planned a
special treasure hunt to propose to my wife. I spoke
with my sister-in-law to help me place all the hints in
the house and we planned that amazing day. I recall
how astonished and excited my wife was when she
discovered her engagement ring, her hidden treasure.
In similar manner, the Creator of heaven and earth has
placed treasures within each person, more valuable and
precious than money, material possession, or worldly
desires. It's as King Solomon once said, *"It is the glory*

of God to conceal a matter, but the glory of kings is to search out a matter" (Proverbs 25:2). It's God's duty to hide His purpose within man, but it's our mission to search it out and discover it.

Graveyard

Do you know that a cemetery is the most barren place on earth? The cemetery is a graveyard filled with the dead treasures of inventions, books, songs, discover-

> *The Creator has deposited hidden treasures within man to enable him to live an extraordinary life on earth.*

ies, cures for diseases, and dreams that never came to existence because people died without discovering God's hidden treasure in their lives. It's heartbreaking to know that every day, thousands and thousands of people are dying without discovering who they are. The Creator has deposited hidden treasures within man to enable him to live an extraordinary life on earth. Yet, it's your responsibility to discover it and access it. In this chapter, we will discover the four hidden treasures that God placed within His creation.

BREATH OF LIFE

The first treasure that God placed in you is the breath of life. Let's look at Genesis 2:7:

> The Lord God formed man of the dust of the ground, and breathed into his nostrils the breath of life; and man became a living being.

God created the firmament, the moon, the sun, the seas, and the vegetation with the words of His mouth. Anything that God spoke into existence is limited to His words and is incapable of moving outside of its identity. For example, the sun only provides sunlight in the day, the moonlight at night, or a tree can only bear fruit according to its kind. Man is the only creature created by God who has a free will to choose his destiny. God, as the Creator of the universe, had the legal right to create man with a word, or a phrase, yet He decided to use His own hands and made mankind in His image and likeness, then breathed into his nostrils the breath of life.

Power to Create

God's creation possesses within it the power and authority to create with the breath of His mouth. Psalms 33:6 says, *"By the word of the Lord the heavens were made, and all the host of them by the breath of His mouth."* The psalmist explains that by the breath of His mouth the earth was created, meaning that the breath that God breathed into man's nostrils is the exact breath that God used to create the earth. That means that the Creator deposited within His creation the power to create.

Creation has the power to bring something from the realm of the invisible to the realm of the visible. You can create something visible from the invisible. God first saw creation before He spoke it into existence. Creating is connected to vision. Dr. David Yonggi Cho says in his book *Successful Home*

> *The Creator deposited within His creation the power to create.*

Cell Groups that visions and dreams are the language of the Holy Spirit [1] (see Joel 2:28). Therefore, the only way you can bring God's kingdom to earth is by visions and dreams. A Believer in Christ will never grow beyond his or her vision. Proverbs 29:18 says, *"Where there is no vision, the people perish."* A life without vision is a life without purpose. For you to fulfill your purpose in life, there must be vision. Remember, creation has the power to bring something from the invisible realm to the visible realm. Therefore, an act of faith is required for creation to be activated. Let's look at some examples:

- *The Wright's brother created the first successful aircraft after observing and studying how birds fly.*

- *Moses built the tabernacle by a pattern shown to him on the mountain* (Exodus 25:40).

- *Nehemiah rebuilt the wall of Jerusalem when he heard of and saw the condition of the wall* (Nehemiah 1).

Someone's vision created and brought into existence everything that surrounds us, such as the beautiful houses or buildings you see every day, the cell phone you use to communicate, and the cars you use for transportation. All of these started with someone who envisioned it and brought it to existence.

In the year 2017, I fasted for seven days. During the fast, the LORD spoke to me and said, "*You will have a son, and his name will be Joshua Caleb.*" My wife and I had been trying for over a year to have a child, but she couldn't get pregnant. So, after I finished the fast, I met with my wife and told her, "*Babe, you will conceive a child, and his name will be Joshua Caleb.*" I laid my hands over my wife's belly, and I prophesied and declared the words over my child's life. Finally, after almost a year my son Joshua Caleb was born. If the Lord has spoken a word over your life or gave promises that haven't come to fruition, remember that inside of you is the breath to create and to bring something from the invisible to the visible realm. The Lord created the earth with His breath of life; now it is your turn to create your life according to His will. You possess in your mouth the power to create your destiny. Before you continue, take a few minutes and begin to create the promises of God over your own life.

The Life of Lucifer

Lucifer was known as the "Son of the Morning." Let's look at some interesting descriptions of Lucifer before his rebellion against heaven (see Isaiah 14 and Ezekiel 28):

- *He dwelt in the presence and throne of God.*
- *He was considered the worship leader in heaven.*
- *He was covered in beauty and splendor.*
- *He was full of wisdom.*

Lucifer had everything a Believer may desire. He had wisdom and riches, he worshiped the Creator, carried God's glory, and dwelt in God's throne in His presence. Lucifer left all splendors, glory, and position and rebelled against the Lord because he yearned to be like God. Instead, God created us in His image and likeness, and gave us the power to create our own destiny. The enemy had everything except the power to create, and the Creator has deposited this power within man. That's why the enemy hates us so much because we have everything that he wished and desired for himself.

Dominion and Authority

The breath of life gives us dominion and authority over the earth. When God made man, He made them to have authority over the entire earth. Let's look at some examples in the Bible:

- *Adam had the capability to name all animal species; he also had the capability to remember them* (Genesis 2:20).

- *Joshua, as a leader of the Israelites, commanded the moon and the sun to stand still until the Israelites defeated the Amorites* (Joshua 10:13).

- *The prophet Elijah said to King Ahab in 1 Kings 17:1, "As the Lord God of Israel lives, before whom I stand, there shall not be dew nor rain these years, **except at my word**,"* and in the same manner, Elijah commanded the heaven to rain (Read 1 King 18:41-45).

- *Peter was able to walk on water at the command of Jesus* (Matthew 14:22-33).

- *Jesus rebuked the wind and the waves, and the storm calmed* (Matthew 8:23-27).

Wow, aren't you excited to know that you have the power and authority over the earth? The LORD gave us all the authority over the earth. Yet, authority releases only if you are under authority. A man or woman who is unsubmissive to his or her earthly authority of ministers, parents, bosses, or government officials will never have authority on earth. To become a man or woman of authority, you must submit and obey your authorities (see Romans 13:1). Remember, all authority is given by

God, not by man. And to be a man of authority, you have to submit to authority.

Power of Life and Death

Death and life are in the power of your breath. Proverbs 18:21 says, *"Death and life are in the power of the tongue."* Man's mouth is a weapon that can bring life or death to a situation. Let's briefly look at some important keys about our words:

- *A Believer has the power to bind or loose in heaven and on earth* (Matthew 18:18-19).

- *Jesus spoke to the diseased and those under demonic possession, and they were healed* (Matthew 8:16).

- *Every idle word a person speaks will be judged on judgment day* (Matthew 12:36).

- *Ezekiel was able to prophesy life to the dry bones, and they became alive* (Ezekiel 37:1-14).

- *The words of a person's mouth have the power to curse or to bless* (James 3:10).

We all heard or saw the news about the tragic helicopter accident involving Kobe Bryant. I was shocked when I heard about his death. I remember watching the players celebrating Kobe's legacy on TV, and what caught my attention was what his NBA friend Tracy McGrady said about him. Tracy said that Kobe always told him that he wanted to die young.[2] It broke my heart to see how Bryant prophesied his own death. And many times, we underestimate the words that come out of our mouth, forgetting that life and death are in the power of the tongue.

> *Man's mouth is a weapon that can bring life or death to a situation.*

One of my nephews shared with me that he struggles with thoughts of suicide because his mom spoke words of death upon his life. I felt heart broken when he shared his heart with me. How many kids are in the same or worse situations than my nephew because someone used the breath of life to bring death instead of life? If you who are reading this have been affected by the use of death words, I would like for you to take few minutes and renounce any negative words or curses spoken over your life. Then begin to speak life to those things that are dead in your life. Don't look at yourself the way people perceive you, look at yourself the way God designed you. Remember, he who is in Christ Jesus is a new creation. The old man has passed away, and all things have become new.

BLUEPRINT

The second treasure that God has placed in man is a blueprint. According to the Merriam-Webster dictionary, a "blueprint" is simply *a detailed plan or program of action*.[3] Every individual on earth is born with a specific detailed plan or program of action inside of them, and the only One Who knows the blueprint of our lives

> *God is known as the architect Who is responsible for designing the blueprint of our lives.*

is our Creator. God is known as the architect Who is responsible for designing the blueprint of our lives. Therefore, it's your responsibility to execute God's plan for your life. Let's read what the LORD has to say about our plans in Jeremiah 29:11 (NIV):

> "For I know the plans I have for you," declares the Lord, "plans to prosper you and not to harm you, plans to give you hope and a future."

The LORD has a specific plan in your life, and His desire is to prosper you on earth. However, the LORD doesn't prosper a person who walks outside of the design that he or she was created to walk in. Any person who walks outside of God's design is automatically out of God's will, and everything outside of God's will eventually dies.

For example, if a fish is out of the water, it dies because the fish was created to swim under the water. If a tree is uprooted from the ground, it will dry up and die because a tree was created to be planted before it can bear fruit. If a person doesn't walk in alignment to God's purpose in their lives, their life will eventually lead to destruction.

Release Your Maximum Potential

The construction of your life must be in alignment with God's eternal plan in order to unleash your maximum potential. For example, let's say that God creates a person to become a doctor in order to save lives through medicine and surgery, but instead they decide to pursue the career of an entrepreneur. That individual may even succeed as an entrepreneur, however, that person will never flourish to his or her maximum potential. You shouldn't live your life out of the desires of your heart because it may lead you to destruction. Let me clarify something: being good at or passionate about something doesn't determine God's blueprint in your life. A person's blueprint is determined by the Creator. If you desire to see the glory of God operating in your life, begin to walk in God's original design for your life.

Criticism

Criticism is a tool the enemy will use to cause you to deviate from God's plan for your life. Therefore, walking in alignment with God will attract criticism. The enemy will use people in your life (such as friends, family members, spouse, and other Believers) to criticize and judge God's original design for your life.

David was anointed for kingship by the prophet Samuel at a very young age. David knew the plans that the LORD had for him, yet his

> *Criticism will be a doorway to draw you closer to God's plans.*

brothers and close relatives saw him as a simple shepherd. At the moment that David faced the giant Goliath, instead of receiving encouragement from his brothers, he was criticized by them. David ignored the criticisms and stood firm in his identity in God. Criticism didn't drive David away from God's plan, instead, it drew him closer to it. Don't let criticism define who you are, but let God be the one to define you. The biggest distinction between King Saul and David was that David always knew God's blueprint for his life, while Saul tried to run away from his design (see I Samuel 10:20-23). When you understand God's blueprint in your life, criticism will be a doorway to draw you closer to God's plans.

Extraordinary Life

The blueprint that God placed in a person's life is to live an extraordinary life. The dictionary defines "extraordinary" as *going beyond what is usual, regular, or customary*.⁴ Some of the antonyms of the word extraordinary are common, normal, usual, and ordinary. The Creator didn't create mankind to live a normal, usual, or common life. On the other hand, He has placed a specific detailed plans inside of man to live an extraordinary life on earth.

In the Bible is a well-known story of Gideon. Gideon was from the tribe of Manasseh, and his was known as the weakest clan. Also, he was considered the least of his father's house. Gideon was living an ordinary life until the angel of the LORD appeared to him and revealed God's purpose for his life. Let's read what the angel of the LORD told Gideon in Judges 6:12, 14:

> ¹²"The LORD is with you, you mighty man of valor!" ¹⁴ Then the Lord turned to him and said, "Go in this might of yours, and you shall save Israel from the hand of the Midianites. Have I not sent you?"

Many people live their lives as Gideon, content with their style of living. They allow society, culture, or custom to define their future and become captive to a system. However, it's when God reveals a person's purpose that they begin walking an extraordinary life.

When I came to Christ, I struggled to search for God's purpose for my life. I finally began to understand when one day, the LORD spoke to my spirit and said, "*I will use you as an epistler on earth to write books.*" That day, my entire life changed because I was able to come into an understanding of God's plan for my life. You could never imagine the greatness of the plans that God has for your life (see Isaiah 55:8-9).

Association

One of the most important keys to discovering the design of God in your life is to associate with someone who has a similar purpose to yours. Let's look at what prevented Abraham from unleashing God's plan for his life in Genesis 12:1-2,4:

> [1] Now the Lord had said to Abram: "Get out of your country, from your family and from your father's house, to a land that I will show you. [2] I will make you a great nation; I will bless you and make your name great; and you shall be a blessing." [4] So Abram departed as the Lord had spoken to him, and Lot went with him. And Abram was seventy-five years old when he departed from Haran.

God commanded Abram to leave his family and go to an unknown country. When we read the story, we see that Abram partially obeyed God because he allowed one of his relatives, Lot, to go with him. The Hebrew word for

Lot is "lowt," which means *a covering or a veil*.[5] Abram was shown the Promised Land the moment he got rid of the veil (the veil represented by Lot; see Genesis 13:14-15).

Lot was considered a righteous man, so righteous that he was willing to give his virgin daughters to the town people of Sodom and Gomorrah in order to protect the visitors, who were actually angels that came to deliver him and his family from God's judgment (see Genesis 19). Although Lot was righteous, he was a veil to Abram preventing him from reaching his destiny.

Walking with people with a dissimilar design to yours could become a stumbling block to you later on in your life. At times, there will be righteous people surrounding you that will become a veil, delaying God's plan in your life. God isn't going to show you your destiny until the veils are removed.

I went through a phase in my walk with Christ when it seemed that I wasn't growing. God taught me that I was stagnant because I was spending my time with the wrong people. The people that I was spending my time with were righteous people, however, they were not part of my blueprint. One of the reasons a person doesn't grow is because of the people he or she spends time with. The Bible states that *"evil company corrupts good habits"* (1 Corinthians 15:33b). Good habits are formed by spending time with individuals with good habits, and bad habits are formed in similar manner, as the Scripture says in Proverbs 27:17, *"As iron sharpens iron, So a man sharpens the countenance of his friend."* Your life is sharpened by the people with whom you surround yourself. Now I understand why my father always told me to choose my friends wisely. Take a moment to pray and identify the "Lots" in your life and remove them from your blueprint.

God's Timing

One of the hardest things to do is to wait on God's timing. When a person tries to accomplish something before God's time, he will be delaying or preventing the plans that God has for his life. Let's look at a few examples:

- *At the age of twelve, Jesus was in the synagogue discussing scriptures in the temple. However, He first had to submit to his parents and wait for God's time to fulfill God's plans for His life. Jesus prepared himself for thirty years to minister for only three and a half years to have the most successful ministry in history.*

- *King David was anointed at a young age, but he had to wait over 30 years to begin his ministry. It was in the wilderness that David's character was molded.*

- *Moses trained 40 years in Egypt, then 40 years in the wilderness. At the age of 80, God called Moses from the midst of the burning bush.*

We need to learn to enjoy the journey of God in our lives, which for some will be short and for others long, but we will see the greatest fruition when we can wait patiently for the call of God in our lives.

ETERNITY

The third treasure God placed in man is eternity. Let's read what Ecclesiastes 3:11a says about eternity, "*He has made everything beautiful in its time. Also He has put eternity in their hearts.*" God has placed eternity in man's heart because eternity is

> *God's original plan was for mankind to dwell with Him in eternity.*

the realm where God dwells and operates. Isaiah 57:15a says, "*For thus says the High and Lofty One who inhabits eternity.*" God's original plan was for mankind to dwell with Him in eternity for He longs to have everlasting communion and fellowship with His creation.

Driven Out of Eternity

As I mentioned earlier, sin separated mankind from God, which resulted in mankind being driven out from eternity. Let's read Genesis 3:9 to see what happened after

Adam and Eve ate of the forbidden tree: *"Then the LORD God called to Adam and said to him, 'Where are you?'"* God is omnipresent, which makes me wonder why He asked Adam where he was in the Garden of Eden. First, we must understand that when God created Adam and Eve, they both were dwelling in the realm of eternity, and they were driven out because of sin. When God asked Adam, *"Where are you?"* In my own words, God's answer to him would have been something like the following: *"Adam, why aren't you dwelling with Me in the eternal realm that I created you to dwell in, where are you?"*

After Adam sinned, he wasn't in the realm of eternity where He created him to dwell. Remember, God inhabits eternity, and Adam and Eve were dwelling in the realm of eternity with Him. However, sin brought an instant separation between man and his Creator removing Adam out of the realm of eternity. Let's look in the book of Isaiah 59:2, when a person sinned against God:

> But your iniquities have separated you from your God, and your sins have hidden His face from you so that He will not hear.

This clearly shows that God doesn't dwell where there's sin or iniquity, and He made it very clear that He won't hear us if there is sin or iniquity in our lives. For instance, why was Lucifer cast out of Heaven, or why was Adam and Eve driven out of Eden? Because iniquity and sin was found in them. If you really desire your prayers to be answered, make sure there isn't any hidden sin or iniquity, and if there is any sin in your life, go and humble yourself before Him and confess your sin, because He is faithful to forgive your sins and restore you.

Eternity is Knowing God

The word "eternity" in the dictionary means *a state to which time has no application, timelessness;*[6] *duration without beginning or end.*[7] In the realm of eternity, time doesn't exist. When it comes to eternity there is a misconception. Many people think of eternity as something futuristic, yet eternity is accessible now. So, how did Jesus define eternal life? Let's read John 17:3, "*This is eternal life, that they may know You, the only true God, and Jesus Christ whom You have sent.*" The Greek word for "know" that is used in the above scriptures is the same word used in the previous chapter, "ginosko," which means *sexual intercourse between a man and a woman.*[8] When you, as a Believer, have an intimate relationship with God, you become one with Him. At this point, you have access and entry to the realm of eternity. Let's look at some examples in the Bible:

- *Abraham was able to intercede in the future judgment on Sodom and Gomorrah. The LORD spoke to Abraham as a friend and revealed His plan of destruction over Sodom and Gomorrah* (see Genesis 19).

- *Noah was able to enter the realm of eternity when God revealed to him the destruction to come upon the earth and told him to build an ark* (see Genesis 6).

- *Moses wrote the first five books of the Bible; how then he was able to write the day of his death? Because Moses was able to enter the realm of eternity* (see Deuteronomy 34:5).

- *Jesus was able to know that Judas Iscariot will betray Him, and who His twelve disciples were going to be. Jesus' oneness with God allowed Him to have full access to the realm of eternity* (see John 13;18-30; Mark 3:13-19).

I was able to know the gender and the name of my first-born son, months before he came into existence. Why? Because God gave mankind access to the realm of eternity. Jesus broke the veil on Calvary and once again gave mankind access to eternity with the Father. It will take intimacy with the Holy Spirit of God to enter the realm of eternity. There are revelations and mysteries that the LORD wants to show you, but it will require you to seek Him intimately. God is waiting to be found by you if you seek Him with all your heart (see Jeremiah 29:13).

GLORY

The final treasure we'll be discussing is the glory that
God has place in every person. To understand this last
treasure God places in mankind, let's read Genesis 2:21-
22 to understand how everything began:

> ²¹ And the Lord God caused a deep sleep to fall on
> Adam, and he slept; and He took one of his ribs, and
> closed up the flesh in its place. ²² Then the rib which
> the Lord God had taken from man He made into a
> woman, and He brought her to the man.

After Adam finished with his assignment of naming every
living creature, the LORD said in Genesis 2:18b, 20b:

> ¹⁸ It is not good that man should be alone; I will make
> him a helper comparable to him. ²⁰ But for Adam there
> was not found a helper comparable to him.

The LORD points out the necessity of a helper in Adam's
life. So, the LORD created the woman from a man's rib.
When God created the woman, He didn't create her to
play an inferior role to that of a man's. Yet, God made
a woman with the most important role, and that is to

be a man's helper. Many women don't like the fact that they're called to be the helper of man because it makes them look inferior to man, but a woman must understand that she is compared to the most important person on earth—the Holy Spirit of God. Jesus said that He had to ascend to heaven in order to send us the Helper, referring to the Holy Spirit. The church needs the Holy Spirit to operate, and the man needs the woman to unleash his glory. The Holy Spirit is the most important person on earth that helps all Christians in their walk. Let's take a look at the following examples:

- *Without the Holy Spirit, Mary wouldn't have conceived the Messiah.*

- *Without the Holy Spirit, Jesus wouldn't be able to perform the work of the Father or be resurrected from death.*

- *Without the Holy Spirit the church in the book of Acts wouldn't have been established.*

- *Without the Holy Spirit, a Christian Believer won't be able to fulfill God's purpose on earth.*

Glory of Man

When God created Adam, the beginning of a woman was inside of him. Nevertheless, Adam couldn't recognize what he had until the LORD took it out of him. So,

what does a woman represent according to the Apostle
Paul in 1 Corinthians 11:7?:

> For a man indeed ought not to cover his head, since
> he is the image and glory of God, but a woman is the
> glory of man.

This verse illustrates that woman is the glory of man.
Adam had a glory (woman) inside of him that only God
knew about. In other words, what God placed in Adam
(or mankind) was glory. Likewise, God has placed a glory
in your life before the foundation of the earth to help
you accomplish the purposes that He has for your life.

Sleeping Condition

For you to manifest
God's glory in your life,
you must die to self.
Before God took Eve
from within Adam, He
put Adam into a state
of deep sleep. In the

*God has placed a glory in
your life before the foundation of the earth to
help you accomplish the
purposes that He has for
your life.*

Bible, the term "*sleep*" may also be used in reference to
a person being dead (see Acts 13:36; Luke 8:52-53; John
11:12-13). A dead person doesn't have any type of feelings,
nor do they have any consciousness; as a matter of fact,
a person could speak rashly to one who is dead or even

hit a dead body and that body won't feel or know a thing. When a person dies to himself, he unleashes the glory the LORD has placed within him. In order for God to unleash His glory upon our generation, we must die to ourselves completely, and this means to die to ourselves daily.

Paul and Silas

Paul and Silas were arrested and thrown into prison for casting out a spirit of divination. They were both beaten with rods, laying many stripes on them, but that didn't prevent them from worshiping God. During worship, an earthquake shook the foundation of the prison and opened every door and loosened every prisoner's chains (see Acts 16:16-40). The enemy thought that he had Paul and Silas captive, but what the enemy didn't realize was that God placed Paul and Silas in prison was so that the keeper of the prison may know about Jesus. Maybe you're in a situation as Paul and Silas, a place of captivity, or a place that seems hopeless, but you're the key for those around you to meet Jesus. Remember, what the LORD has placed in your life is a glory that will shake the kingdom of darkness. The glory that God has placed in your life isn't only for yourself, but for those around you that need to be set free and hear about Jesus.

Stephen the Martyr

Stephen, a man full of the Holy Spirit, preached the gospel boldly without the fear of dying for Christ. Stephen was stoned to death, yet it was in this moment that he was able to see heaven open and see the glory of God (see Acts 7:54-56). If you want to see the glory of God in your life, our flesh must be crucified, and we must die daily.

Stephen made one of the most powerful remarks in the Bible before dying. He said, "*Lord, do not charge them with this sin*" (Acts 7:60b). After, being stoned to death, he asked the LORD not to charge them with their sin. Are you willing to do the same thing for those who criticize you, curse you, and plan evil against you? Are you willing to sacrifice your life for them? I don't know if you realize that Saul was a witness to and part of the reason Stephen was murdered. God heard Stephen's prayer and transformed Saul into the Apostle Paul that we know today. Dying to yourself means that we no longer use "I" in our vocabulary. Our only focus is God's will and no longer ours.

Surgery

Adam had to "die" first and have a surgical procedure by God Himself in order to release the glory that was inside of him. Many people want to release the glory of God in their lives, but few want to go through the refining process. The process will leave you with a scar that will glorify God. Let's look at some examples:

- *Jacob's wounded hip after the struggle with God* (Genesis 32:22-32)

- *Paul's thorn in the flesh* (2 Corinthians 12:6-7)

- *Jesus' pierced hands and feet* (Luke 23:33-34)

I'm not going to sell you a dream and tell you that it's going to be easy. No one likes the refining process. However, it's the only way we're going to see the glory of the LORD manifest in our lives. It's a hard process, but a most rewarding one.

God's Presence

Moses asked the LORD, "*Please, show me Your glory,*" and the LORD response was, "*You cannot see My face; for no man shall see Me, and live*" (Exodus 33:18, 20). If we want to see the glory of the LORD in our lives, we must be ready to die daily and allow the Creator to bring us into His refining process. Nevertheless, the only way a Believer can die daily in the flesh is if He spends time in the presence of God. I wrote about the four treasures that the Creator has placed within man, but without His presence we would never have fully accessed to those deposits. I would like to conclude with this statement: desire the presence of God more than spiritual gifts or manifestation and more than your family, work, and ministry. Let the presence of God take preeminence in your daily walk, and you'll be able to experience the hand of the LORD upon your life. The Scripture says the following:

> **Seek first the kingdom of God and His righteousness, and everything else will be added to you.**
>
> **—Matthew 6:33**

Seeking the LORD is like playing treasure hunt. Every clue you find draws you closer to Him. The closer you draw to Him, the hungrier you become for His presence. Remember, the treasures that God placed in His creation weren't given to be buried, but rather to reveal His glory.

TREASURE HUNT

In this chapter, we discover the four hidden treasures that the Creator placed in mankind before the foundation of the earth.

REVIEW QUESTIONS

1. According to Genesis 2:7, what did God breath into man's nostrils?

    _____

    _____

    _____

2. Read Psalm 33:6, and write in your own words, how you feel knowing that God placed the power and authority inside of you to create with the breath of His mouth.

    _____

    _____

    _____

3. According to Proverbs 18:21, why are the words we speak so important, and how can it affect someone?

    _____

    _____

4. According to Jeremiah 29:11, what does God have for you?

_____

_____

_____

5. According to Ecclesiastes 3:11, what has God placed in the heart of man?

_____

_____

_____

PERSONAL QUESTIONS

1. What kind of negative words have people around you spoken over you? Write them down, then I would like for you to take few minutes and renounce any negative words or curses spoken over your life.

_____

_____

_____

_____

Note: Don't let the words around you destroy you, however, let the Word of God build and edify you.

2. Do you know God's purpose in your life? If not, how difficult has it been to walk without purpose?

_____

_____

_____

Note: Don't feel discouraged if you haven't discovered your life purpose. I know how difficult it is to walk without purpose. As you build a relationship with God, you will begin to discover your life purpose.

3. Why is knowing your life blueprint extremely important, and how can it help you?

_____

_____

_____

4. What is the purpose of the glory that God placed in your life?

_____

_____

_____

Prayer Time: Let's take a moment and pray that God will help us discover the hidden treasure in our life.

Heavenly Father,

The Scripture says that "it is the glory of God to conceal a matter, but the glory of kings is to search out a matter" (Proverbs 25:2). Father, it's Your duty to hide treasure within man, but it's our responsibility to search it out and discover it. I pray that You will help me discover and unleash everything you have placed within me. Help me discover the hidden treasure in my life that will reveal Your glory. In the precious name of Jesus Christ I pray.

Amen

CHAPTER 8

What Is In Your Hand?

So the LORD said to him, "What is that in your hand?" He said, "A rod."

—Exodus 4:2

IN THE SUMMER OF 2015, I was in the church sanctuary, desperately crying before the LORD, asking Him what my life's purpose is—for what was I created? I was tired of being an ordinary Christian. I knew deep inside of me that I was called for something greater. While I was praying, the Spirit of God spoke to me, and asked, *"What do you have in your hands?"*

I replied, *"A pen."*

He told me, *"I will use you as an epistler on earth to write books."*

When I heard those words, I began to cry like a newborn baby. The answer that I was searching for my entire life was always within my reach. What you're looking for isn't in the deepest part of the ocean, or in the highest mountain, neither is it found on the other side of the world. What you're looking for isn't far away, it's so close that, it's within your reach. When you discover what the LORD placed in your hands, it will empower you to carry out God's purpose in your life.

PROVISION

The first benefit of knowing what God has placed in your hand is provision. The provision that you need to fulfill God's assignment on earth is in your possession; all you need to do is find it. A perfect example of God's provision is the story of a widow found in the book of 2 Kings:

> [1] A certain woman of the wives of the sons of the prophets cried out to Elisha, saying, "Your servant my husband is dead, and you know that your servant feared the Lord. And the creditor is coming to take my two sons to be his slaves." [2] So Elisha said to her, "What shall I do for you? Tell me, what do you have in the house?" And she said, "Your maidservant has nothing in the house but a jar of oil." – 2 Kings 4:1-2

After her husband died, this widow went through an economic crisis in which she didn't have enough money to pay the creditor. As a result, the creditors were going to take her two sons. The widow desperately sought help from the Prophet Elisha, a man of God. And it's interesting that Elisha didn't pray over her finances or ask God to pour out money from heaven. Instead, Elisha asked the widow, *"Tell me, what do you have in the house?."* So, how did the man of God help the poor widow? By directing her to the resources she already had in her house.

The resources that the widow needed to solve her crisis were always inside the house. The problem with the widow is that she wasn't able to recog-

> **What the LORD has placed in your hand will be the tool for your provision.**

nize it. Oftentimes we want God to miraculously deposit $40,000 in our bank account to solve all our financial problems. Yet, all He desires is that you begin to utilize what He has placed in your hand to bless you. Probably the resources that you need to be financially free have been hidden for years under your bed or in your closet, or it's in your house filled with dust, having always been in your possession and you didn't realize it.

Did you know that the multimillion dollar companies such as: Amazon, Disney, Google, and Microsoft all began their business in the garage of a house or in a dorm room? Maybe all you need is a homemade food recipe to open your restaurant, or a computer to start a business, or a piece of clothing to become a designer. What you need to solve your crisis is already within your reach. Remember, what the LORD has placed in your hand will be the tool for your provision.

EMPOWERMENT

The second benefit of knowing what God has placed in your hands is empowerment. God will use what He has placed in your hands to empower you to perform His work. Exodus 4:2-4 tells us how the LORD empowered Moses to perform His work:

> [2] So the Lord said to him, "What is that in your hand?" He said, "A rod." [3] And He said, "Cast it on the ground." So he cast it on the ground, and it became a serpent; and Moses fled from it. [4] Then the Lord said to Moses, "Reach out your hand and take it by the tail" (and he reached out his hand and caught it, and it became a rod in his hand).

As recorded in the Scriptures, Moses is the only survivor of the massacre Pharaoh decreed on all male children born. He knew inside of himself that he was not born by casualty, but the LORD had a special plan for his life. One day, Moses saw an Egyptian beating a Hebrew, and he tried to fix the situation by killing and hiding him in the sand. Here, we see how Moses tried to liberate the Israelites with his own strength. Therefore, Moses feared and fled to the land of Midian. There, he became a shepherd for

> *God will use what He has placed in your hands to empower you to perform His work.*

40 years. Notice that for 40 years he had a supernatural rod in his possession that he never knew he had until it was revealed to him. However, before the LORD revealed the supernatural rod to Moses, he first had to pass through a season of 40 years to mold his character.

Supernatural Rod

After Moses' encounter with the LORD at the burning bush, the LORD asked him what he had in his hand, and his response was, *"A rod."* God gave Moses a rod to perform His works. Let's look at some of the work Moses was able to perform:

- *Plagues in front of Pharaoh* (Exodus 4:17, 21)

- *Divide the Red Sea* (Exodus 14:21)

- *Turn the river into blood* (Exodus 7:17, 18, 20)

- *Make water come out of a rock* (Exodus 17:5-6)

The rod was a simple wooden stick. There was nothing magical or special about it, but once Moses surrendered it to God, it became a supernatural rod. How can something that was insignificant and dead become so powerful? When you surrender what God has placed in your hands to Him, it will become the most powerful weapon or tool. God empowered Moses with a rod to perform His works. God has empowered you with your own unique rod to perform His work.

Every person has a calling in his life, but few possess the character to fulfill it. God allows certain seasons in our lives to shape our character for us to fulfill our

> *When you surrender what God has placed in your hands to Him, it will become the most powerful weapon or tool.*

calling. I had supernatural pens and pencils in my hands since the time I was in kindergarten all the way through college that I never knew I had until the LORD revealed it to me, and this will empower me to reveal God's glory. There are things in your life that you have been using for years that seem insignificant, and God is going to use them to empower you to release His glory.

DESTINATION

The third benefit of knowing what God has placed in your hands is how it will position you to reach your destination. Let's look at the story of David. David was anointed king by Prophet Samuel at a young age, but what positioned David to reach his destination as king of Israel was what God placed in his hands.

Harp

The first thing God placed in his hands was a simple harp. Let's read from 1 Samuel 16:21-23 how the harp positioned David for his purpose:

> [21] So David came to Saul and stood before him. And he loved him greatly, and he became his armorbearer. [22] Then Saul sent to Jesse, saying, "Please let David stand before me, for he has found favor in my sight." [23] And so it was, whenever the spirit from God was upon Saul, that David would take a harp and play it with his hand. Then Saul would become refreshed and well, and the distressing spirit would depart from him.

The harp positioned David to be King Saul's armorbearer. Every time David played the harp, the distressing spirit would depart from Saul. The harp wasn't a special instrument, but the one that was playing the harp was anointed by God. Every time David played, the anointing would flow over his hands into the harp. The LORD has anointed your hands to release His glory, but all He's waiting for is for you to place your hands on the correct instrument and start playing.

Sling and Stone

The second thing God placed in David's hands was a sling and stones. Let's look at what the Scripture says in 1 Samuel 17:49-50:

> [49] Then David put his hand in his bag and took out a stone; and he slung it and struck the Philistine in his forehead, so that the stone sank into his forehead, and he fell on his face to the earth. [50] So David prevailed over the Philistine with a sling and a stone, and struck the Philistine and killed him.

David was too young to be qualified as a soldier; neither had he the necessary training. However, David had a tested sling in his hands that he used to kill a bear and a lion. When David faced the giant, Goliath, he didn't fear the giant

What God places within your hands will position you to reach your destination.

because David knew what God had placed in his hands. David didn't only kill Goliath but was positioned as a captain over a thousand men. What God placed in David positioned him on the course of his destination, to become king of Israel. Remember, what God places within your hands will position you to reach your destination.

VICTORY

The last benefit is the victory that will be brought into your life by what God has placed in your hands. Why did Moses come out victorious against Pharaoh? Because the LORD put a rod in Moses' hands. In Judges 15:16, Samson said:

> With the jawbone of a donkey, Heaps upon heaps, With the jawbone of a donkey I have slain a thousand men!

Samson was able to kill a thousand men with the jawbone of a donkey in his hands. David was also able to kill the giant Goliath with a simple sling

When you discover what the LORD has placed in your hands, it will enable you to come out victorious.

and a stone because he knew what God had placed in his hands. What the LORD has placed in your hands isn't only to bring provision or to empower you to perform

His works, but to destroy the works of the enemy. When you discover what the LORD has placed in your hands, it will enable you to come out victorious.

Your Hands

There was always a woman inside of Adam of which he wasn't aware until God revealed it to him. The widow had a jar of oil that she never paid attention to. Moses had a rod that he walked with and didn't know that God was going to use it to perform miraculous works. In your hands, you possess the tool to release God's glory in your life. All you must do is discover it and surrender it to Him.

WHAT IS IN YOUR HAND?

The purpose of this chapter is to help you discover the tools that God has placed in your hands to reveal His glory.

REVIEW QUESTIONS

1. According to 2 Kings 4:1-2, what did the widow have in her house?

_____

_____

_____

2. What kind of signs was Moses able to perform in Egypt with his rod?

_____

_____

_____

3. In your own words, write how the sling and the stone helped David to be promoted.

_____

_____

_____

4. According to Judges 15:16, what was in Samson's hand to destroy the enemy?

_____

_____

PERSONAL QUESTION

1. Can you describe in your own words what God has placed in your hands? And how that can help you release God's glory in your life?

_____

_____

_____

_____

_____

_____

CHAPTER 9

Sowing and Reaping

⁷ Do not be deceived, God is not mocked; for whatever a man sows, that he will also reap. ⁸For he who sows to his flesh will of the flesh reap corruption, but he who sows to the Spirit will of the Spirit reap everlasting life.

—Galatians 6:7-8

THERE'S A MUCH LOVED tale that has travelled the world and been greatly exaggerated with the passing of time. Nonetheless, at its core, the story is true, and the message speaks of a timeless principle. The story is as follows:

There was a young man named Howard Kelly who paid his college tuition by selling goods from house to house. There was a day when Howard had no money, not even to buy a piece of bread, and he was hungry. Though not a new experience to Howard, he decided that he would ask for something to eat at the first house he encountered along the way. He then saw a house near a farm and went and knocked at the door of that house. Then, a young and beautiful lady opened the door. Startled and somewhat shy, Howard instead asked for a glass of water. However, the young lady, instead of water, brought Howard a glass of milk.

He slowly drank the glass of milk while conversing with the young lady and then said to her, "*How much do I owe you?*"

The young lady replied, "*You don't owe me anything. Mother taught us never to accept payment for kindness.*"

Years later, that young lady became seriously sick and was taken to a big city hospital to be treated because the local doctors didn't have the resources to treat her illness. Howard Kelly, having become a doctor, was one of the specialists that treated the woman and saved her life. As an act of kindness, Dr. Kelly paid her hospital bill. However, the woman didn't know this and was concerned about how she was going to pay for the hospital bill. When she received the bill, the end of the bill said, *"Paid in full with one glass of milk. (Signed): Dr. Howard Kelly."* [1]

When I first heard this story, I recall being convicted by the Holy Spirit. God spoke to my spirit and said, *"What have you sown in My Kingdom that you could reap?"* I stood silently because I had no answer. At that moment, I understood that you can be a man with many visions and dreams, but if you don't take time to sow into them, then you will never reap a harvest.

Judgment Day

Suppose that in the next few minutes you must appear before the Judgment Seat of Christ. What kind of harvest would you be presenting before the LORD? Everyone on earth must give God an account on judgment day, and it's evident that everyone has received gifts from the LORD as in the parable of the talents. This young lady only sowed a single glass of milk as an act of kindness and received a miracle in return. Before the miracle starts knocking at your door, it must first be sown.

Your Harvest

Through the decades, the body of Christ has benefited from the gifting and anointing of men and women of God who received gifts such as: a prophetic word, a deliverance, healing, or revelation. However, the body of

Christ has become too comfortable and has begun feeding on someone else's harvest, while at the same time neglecting their responsibility to sow and reap their own gifts. Today, God is calling you to sow into His promises over your life because there are people who need to get fed from your harvest. Maybe you're the next Billy Graham who God is going to use to preach the gospel to millions of people. Maybe you're the next worshiper who has songs that will bring heaven to earth. Or perhaps you're the next writer who's going to impact generations through your writing. Within every man, there is harvest, but to reap a harvest, there must first be sowing. In this chapter, I'll be elaborating on the process of sowing and reaping, and the important elements necessary to release God's glory in your life. Let us first understand a few principles about sowing and reaping.

I. YOU ALWAYS REAP WHAT YOU SOW.

- *If you sow apple seeds, you'll reap apples.*
- *Don't expect a harvest if you haven't sown anything.*
- *Your harvest will be the result of your sowing.*

II. YOU ALWAYS REAP MORE THAN WHAT YOU SOW.

- *Sowing activates the law of multiplication.*
- *Your life's productivity is determined by your ability to sow.*

III. YOU ALWAYS REAP AT A DIFFERENT SEASON THAN WHEN YOU SOWED.

- *Every harvest has its own season.*
- *Some seeds bear fruit at different seasons.*
- *Reaping off-season, or out of God's time, will destroy the harvest.*
- *Your season doesn't depend on a man, a minister, or you. Your season only depends on God.*

SEED

First, a seed must be identified. In Genesis 1:12a we read, *"And the earth brought forth grass, the herb that yields seed according to its kind, and the tree that yields fruit, whose seed is in itself according to its kind."* A seed only bears fruit according to its kind, or simply put, according to its DNA. As mentioned before, a pear seed produces pears, apple seeds apples, and orange seeds oranges. You're a vessel called to bear fruit according to the kind of seeds God has sown in you. Let me explain. A seed must first be sown in the earth in order for it to be activated, and just like the earth, we are earthen vessels carrying within us the seeds of God's specific calling in our lives. Therefore, only God, our Creator, knows the kind of seeds we carry.

Discovering Your Identity

Discovering the kind of seeds within you means discovering your identity. Your identity defines you and gives meaning to your existence on earth. It's important to understand that a person who has realized his or her identity has a strong foundation in life. This is one of the main reasons why Jesus couldn't be moved, for He knew who He was on Earth, and having realized His identity caused Him to have a solid foundation during His life.

On one occasion, Jesus rebuked Peter, one of the twelve disciples, because Peter (rebuking Jesus) stood in the way of Christ's forewarning concerning His crucifixion. Let's look at the account of Matthew concerning this:

> [21] He must go to Jerusalem, and suffer many things from, the elders and chief priest and scribes, and be killed, and be raised the third day. [22] Then Peter took Him aside and began to rebuke Him, saying, "Far be it from You, Lord; this shall not happen to You!" [23] But He turned and said to Peter, "Get behind Me, Satan!"
> —Matthew 16:21-23

A person who knows their identity in Christ won't be moved by the enemy's voice. The rain may descend, the flood may come, and the wind may blow; but if you stand firm on the Rock (Jesus), your life won't be moved (see Matthew 7:24-25). That's why it's extremely important to know what God says about who you are—not what your neighbor, your best friend, or what you believe you are. The Creator sees us the way He created us, and if you desire to produce a harvest in your life, you must first be able to identify the type of seed. Unless you're able to identify your seed, you will never be able to bring forth a harvest.

GROUND

In the principle of sowing and reaping, the next process is to evaluate the ground in which you are sowing. Over 50% of the fruits in the United States are imported due to its land and climate conditions preventing some fruits from being produced.[2] Every kind of seed requires a specific type of ground for it to grow. In the parable of the sower (Matthew 13:1-9; 18-23), all the seeds were of the same kind, but the focus wasn't so much on the type of seed as much as it was about the type of ground on which they fell—this affected the seed's growth in a positive or negative way.

Be Planted in the Right Ground

I can't talk about planting without mentioning Lighthouse Christian Fellowship. This is where the principles of being planted were first laid in my life, amongst many other foundational truths. I can say with certainty that if I'd been planted some other place, at the very least, my faith wouldn't have been strong enough and my spiritual growth would've been stunted. What Lighthouse offers was necessary, essential, and fundamental for my destiny and calling to be realized. I will always thank God for Pastor Roger and this church ministry as a whole. Being planted in the proper soil can lead to history being made, destinies changed, and nations transformed for the glory of God.

Growth

God is responsible for bringing growth into our lives (see 1 Corinthians 3:7). However, God isn't able to bring growth if you aren't planted in the right ground. If an individual is planted in the wrong soil environment, the individual will never grow or reach their maximum potential. For example, a cactus has the ability to grow in the desert, while other plants cannot, because they eventually die due to the kind of ground or ambient conditions. Sadly, there are many people who are spiritually dead because they aren't planted in the right soil.

A faithful, devout Christian may be of a good seed and never harvest a crop because they were in the wrong place. To be planted in the right soil means that the land has the required nutrients and is able to provide a suitable environment for a seed to grow. If you find yourself stagnant and not growing, ask yourself this question, "*In what type of soil am I planted?*" To be planted in fertile ground as a Believer in Christ doesn't necessarily mean that you're going to be in a comfortable place or be free from afflictions and tribulations. To be planted in the right soil means to be in an environment where all the "necessary nutrients" for your growth are present. God may put you in a place where you'll have to go through a fiery furnace, a lion's den, a prison, or through the wilderness for the sole purpose of causing you to grow and bear much fruit for His glory.

The enemy will use offenses as a way to hinder your spiritual growth and cause you to be uprooted from where God purposed for you to be planted. Observe how the cunning serpent caused Adam and Eve to be driven out from the Garden of Eden. This "uprooting" of Adam and Eve led them to a harsh environment as opposed to the perfect one in which the Lord God designed for them to thrive and prosper.

Here are some of the reasons some Believers leave the place God planted them: "I'm not growing spiritually," "I should be leading worship or the youth service." "They are too strict." "There is no order." "I don't agree with how they run the service." "I'm wasting my time here." "Nothing is changing." "My leader doesn't acknowledge me." And the list goes on. Some of these scenarios are legitimate, but many are just excuses we make to justify our fleshly reasoning. The Scripture clearly says, *"Those who are planted in the house of the LORD Shall flourish in the courts of our God"* (Psalm 92:13). First of all, the main question we must ask God is, *"Lord where do you want me to be planted?"* When a person has a clear understanding of where God wants them to be planted, then everything else is secondary. If you are faithful, God Himself will position you, open doors for you, promote you, cause spiritual growth in your life, and provide everything else needed for you to live a fulfilled life. It's extremely important to be planted in good soil in the proper environment, because every good seed needs good ground in order for it to grow.

Joseph

Do you know how Joseph became Pharaoh's right-hand man? Joseph's life was sown in the right soil. If he'd been planted his entire life in Canaan, he'd never have reached the throne. Egypt had all the suitable nutrients for Joseph's growth.

King David

If David wasn't faithful to be planted at his father's house, he wouldn't have been positioned to receive his father's command to send food to his brother at the battlefield, which led to him killing Goliath and eventually becoming the king of Israel.

Through the reading of the Scriptures, I'm pretty sure that David was eager to be part of something bigger, to bring glory to God and victory to Israel. I'm sure he thought many times of being on the battlefield, boasting on His God and using his God-given gifts and abilities for the glory of God and for the love of his people, Israel. But being planted in his father's house taking care of his father's sheep prepared him for how God was going to use him in the future. The testimony of how David killed the lion and the bear, the songs he wrote, sang, and played at his leisure time, the time he would spend reading the Scriptures, was all essential for God to mold and prepare him. From these experiences and personal victories, David drew his faith, strength, and courage. It's good to point out the fact that no one was watching or acknowledging David throughout this period of his life, but when you dwell in the secret place, you will be rewarded in the open.

Planted Versus Buried

It's crucial to know the difference between planting and burying. Both processes of planting and burying involves digging; however, planting brings life and growth, while burying suppresses and hinders growth. A seed is able to grow when it's planted, not when it's buried. It's important to know what seed is being sown because certain seeds require certain planting depths. If you sow a seed too deeply in the ground, you will hinder its ability to grow. Many people bury their dreams, visions, or purpose, and never see growth in their lives because they were never planted. In other words, they never invested themselves into their dreams but remained stagnant and complacent, which is synonymous to burying them (see Psalm 1).

CULTIVATING THE SEED

Cultivation is the most important process for a successful crop. Cultivating is the process by which the farmer provides the necessary care required for the seed to grow and produce fruits. The way a farmer cultivates his crops will determine the productivity of the harvest. In the book of Genesis, God reveals His intended will for Adam to cultivate and keep what He had planted in the Garden of Eden (see Genesis 2:15). Therefore, it's man's responsibility to cultivate his crops as revealed in the Scriptures.

Harvest Time

A good farmer knows that time is crucial to a great harvest. The process of cultivating is similar to that of an investor because they both demand time. Entrepreneurs know that the best investment is a long-term one because short-term investments usually don't guarantee a good return due to its higher risk nature, which becomes more like gambling. However, a long-term investment demands substantial time but usually yields a greater reward.

So, how much time are you investing in your dreams? How much time are you investing in God's promises for your life? In what are you investing your time? Your harvest comes from the place in which your time is being invested. If a person spends his or her time on social media, Netflix, or TV shows, do you know what that person is going to reap? Procrastination. Procrastination is destroying this generation. This generation is spending more time on social media than in God's presence. Let's look at what Paul said to the church of Galatians, "*For he who sows to his flesh will of the flesh reap corruption*" (Galatians 6:8a). Any person who sows in the flesh only reaps losses. Do you know why many Believers in Christ feel dry, dead, or unable to reap anything in their lives? Because they aren't investing time cultivating their crops.

- *If you want to see a happy marriage, invest time in your spouse.*
- *If you want to see a functional home, invest time in your family.*

- *If you want to be a successful entrepreneur, invest time in your business.*
- *If you want to be used powerfully by God, invest time with Him.*
- *If you want to reap God's blessings for your life, invest your time cultivating His promises.*

Like in the parable of the talents, we may often become like the servant who decided to bury his talent, hoping for the talent to miraculously multiply. Let me make this clear, there won't be multiplication without meaningful actions. Faith operates with works, and reaping operates with sowing. God is calling you to begin to cultivate your time in your crops so you may reap your harvest.

REAPING THE HARVEST

The farmer's most joyful moment is the time of harvest. When the time of reaping has finally come, there is exuberant joy after all the labor, sweat, and hard work. Reaping a harvest has two main benefits.

Blessing

The first benefit of reaping a harvest is that it brings abundant blessings. Everyone loves for God to pour out His blessings in their lives, however, God wants everyone to be blessed, not just a few. Therefore, God brings blessings in a person's life, not only for the sake of the individual, but also to be a blessing to others. God wants you to be an instrument in His hands in order for Him to channel and propagate his blessings throughout the world. It's God's will for you to succeed in your life and to fulfill your dreams, whether that's writing a song, creating music, launching a business, building ministries, or becoming an influential leader, all of that has God's full support, and He wants you to know that in His hands it won't corrupt, but bring life and God's blessings to the world. Psalm 24:1a, KJV says, "*The earth is the LORD'S, and the fullness thereof.*" And we also know by the Scriptures that "*It is more blessed to give than to receive*" (Acts 20:35c). Why did God give up His only begotten Son? Because He loved the world, and by giving His Son's life, those that believed in Him will receive eternal life (see John 3:16). God's system of exchange is very different from that of the world. God is the ultimate giver, giving mankind eternal life through Jesus Christ. Reaping a harvest is the result of hard work, but always remember that "*it is more blessed to give than to receive.*"

Multiplication

The second benefit of reaping a harvest is that it brings multiplication. Since the time of Creation, God commanded mankind to multiply. The purpose of multiplication is to expand the Kingdom of God. God has called us to be like Joshua and conquer the Promised Land and expand His kingdom. God isn't only calling you to conquer His promises, but He's calling you to spread His kingdom. He needs available vessels to expand His kingdom in the government, schools, workforce, military, prisons, hospitals, and all over the nations of the world. However, God is waiting for you to begin to sow in the kingdom so you can harvest for His kingdom.

Don't Grow Weary

You may not know at what stage of the process of sowing and reaping you find yourself. Maybe you haven't been able to find your identity, you might be looking for a place to be planted, in the process of cultivating your crop, or in the process of reaping your harvest. Let's always remind ourselves about what the Apostle Paul said in Galatians 6:9, "*Let us not grow weary while doing good, for in due season we shall reap if we do not lose heart.*" Stay in the race, be strong in the Lord, and always believe that He is faithful to fulfill all He has promised.

SOWING AND REAPING

In this chapter, we learn the process of sowing and reaping and the important elements necessary to release God's glory in your life.

REVIEW QUESTIONS

1. According to Psalm 92:13, what happens when you are planted in the house of the LORD?

   _____

   _____

   _____

2. According to 1 Corinthians 3:7, NIV, how are you responsible to bring growth in your life?

   _____

   _____

   _____

3. According to the parable of the sower, what caused the seeds to grow or not to grow? (Read Matthew 13:1-9; 18-23.)

   _____

   _____

   _____

4. What does Acts 20:15 say about giving?

_____

_____

_____

5. According to John 3:16, what example does God give to mankind about giving?

_____

_____

_____

PERSONAL QUESTIONS

1. Why identifying the type of seed in your life is important?

_____

_____

_____

_____

2. How do you see yourself, are you planted or are you buried? Explain why?

_____

_____

_____

_____

3. How are you investing your time in your crop? If you are not, why?

_____

_____

_____

4. How are you being a blessing to others?

_____

_____

Prayer Time: Let's take a moment and pray that God will help us to be planted in the right house.

Heavenly Father,

Your Word says that "Those who are planted in the house of the Lord shall flourish," (Psalm 92:13) and I deeply desire to flourish and reap a harvest for Your Kingdom. God, help me identify and discover the place you desire for me to be planted, so I may grow and produce fruit that will remain for Your Kingdom. Direct and guide my steps into Your perfect plan for my life. In the precious name of Jesus Christ I pray.

Amen

CHAPTER 10

Relay Race

Do you not know that those who run in a race all run, but one receives the prize? Run in such a way that you may obtain it.

—1 Corinthians 9:24

IN 1 CORINTHIANS 9:24, Paul encourages all Believers to run as if they're running a race, that is, running with the intent and purpose of achieving the ultimate prize. Our lives here on earth can be compared to that of a race, pressing forward until we get to the finish line. Likewise, we should constantly be working towards fulfilling the purpose for which we were created by our Heavenly Father. Nevertheless, the reality is a sad one. Not everyone that runs finishes the race they've started, and not everyone fulfills their destiny. It's our responsibility to finish the race we started, but it's crucial to know that our race isn't an independent one, it's a relay race. In other words, we depend on each other to finish and receive our reward.

What Is a Relay Race?

A runner carries a baton and runs a specified distance then hands the baton to the next runner. Passing the baton must take place within a restricted zone, and while the next runner begins to sprint and sync with the runner passing them. So timing is crucial. All of this must happen without dropping the baton. If the runners don't pass the baton within the restricted zone, or if they drop it somewhere along the race, the team is automatically disqualified.

What Does the Baton Symbolize?

Passing the baton symbolizes the transfer of the mantle to the next generation. The

> *The rise or collapse of nations depends on leadership.*

mantle is symbolic of the role of leadership, its vision, spirit, and ministry. To illustrate this more clearly, before Elijah was taken, he successfully passed down his ministry to Elisha, leaving behind his mantle. In response to his faith, Elisha then picked up the mantle and continued the ministry that Elijah started, following in his footsteps and functioning in the same capacity of leadership as Elijah.

The baton is the symbol of leadership. The rise or collapse of nations depends on leadership. Our rights, beliefs, education, economy, morals, and values are all influenced by our leaders. The level of influence a leader has affects families, communities, the workplace, and its country. Ineffective leaders governing and representing our world lack character, morals, values, and good ethics. As a result, the world is negatively impacted. For this reason, before one can successfully pass down the baton, we must disciple true leaders that will faithfully, loyally, and successfully carry out their earthly mission.

The Importance of Discipleship

Discipleship is the means by which leaders are formed. A great discipleship will bring

> *Discipleship is the means by which leaders are formed.*

about great leaders. When Jesus Christ walked on this earth, He trained disciples that were able to continue the work He began during His earthly ministry. What made Jesus' ministry so successful wasn't so much the magnitude of His influence or the immense impact He had on the lives of so many people, but rather His ability to produce disciples that would replicate and continue His work with such effectiveness and success. It has now been about 2,000 years since Jesus Christ walked on this earth, and the work He began still continues to this day. Jesus' ability to pass down His knowledge, experiences, abilities, and leadership qualities to His disciples was like no other.

When we read the Holy Scriptures, we come to understand that the key to Jesus' success is the Holy

> *Discipleship was the fundamental key for the expansion of God's kingdom.*

Spirit. Though He left the earth, He never left His disciples, but bestowed His Spirit upon them. We must understand that Jesus didn't only come to earth to accomplish His assignment on the cross, but to train disciples. Discipleship was the fundamental key for the expansion of God's kingdom. That's why, before He left to return to the Father, He commanded us to train disciples of all nations (see Matthew 28:16-20).

Part of accomplishing God's purpose in your life includes pouring out everything you've received from the Father to the next generation. We are here not only to finish our race but to help those after us finish theirs. Generations have been disqualified because we have put so much emphasis upon running our own race that we have forgotten about passing the baton to the next generation.

Baton Dropped

In the spring break of 2009, upon my return home from college, a tragic event took place in my life during the first week of my arrival. My father was admitted to the hospital and passed away shortly after. This was really unexpected and everything happened so fast that I wasn't able to process the reality of his death. His absence made me wander for many years, and I became as one with no identity and purpose in life. Thankfully, that all changed on the day I had an encounter with Jesus Christ. He turned my mourning into joy. My father was a well-respected man, full of wisdom, and a man of integrity. I personally can say that he raised me well and was a role model to me and my siblings. But he dropped the ball when he finished the race of his life without successfully passing the baton to the next generation, a mistake many parents make. As a result, I had to start from zero, and because of it, I made many unnecessary and repeatable mistakes. My dad failed to give instructions after his passing because he never prepared for his death. Paul said in 2 Timothy 4:6, "*For I am already being poured out as a drink offering, and the time of my departure is at hand.*" Paul was ready to die for Christ which also helped him to prepare and set things in order before his passing.

It Is Finished

The apostle Paul understood that the Christian walk is like a race, hence his exhortation to Timothy, *"I have fought the good fight, I have finished the race, I have kept the faith"* (2 Timothy 4:7). Paul was an example of one who endured and finished the race to the end, successfully passing the baton to his son of faith, Timothy.

Another example of One who finished the race He started is Jesus Christ. Let's look at what Jesus said in the gospel of John 19:30:

> [30] So when Jesus had received the sour wine, He said, "It is finished!" And bowing His head, He gave up His spirit.

Jesus Christ represents the first runner, and the baton has been passed through multiple generations, starting with His twelve disciples. The time of transition has already begun, the baton has been passed to this generation, similar to how it was passed from Moses to Joshua, from David to Solomon, and from Elijah to Elisha. The LORD is entrusting the chosen generation to carry out His will, purpose, and truth on earth. We're at the transitioning point when the baton is being pass. You might be on the receiving end, or perhaps the one passing it. Whatever your position, just be careful to not

drop it. The time is at hand for this generation to finish
the race. Often, we focus so much on ourselves that we
forget about leaving a legacy for the next generation.
The fathers of this generation need to understand the
importance of passing on the baton. In this final chapter,
I will be concluding with the implications of what true
discipleship entails.

TRAINING AND TEACHING

In the most basic sense, discipleship is the process of
teaching and training individuals or a group in some
sort of discipline for their lives. The book of Proverbs
exhorts us thus, "*Train up a child in the way he should
go, and when he is old he will not depart from it*" (Proverbs 22:6). How many times have we heard this verse
being preached by our pastors, leaders, friends, and
parents? When I first read this verse, I only saw one
truth being expressed, which is that parents are in
charge of instructing their children in the ways of the
Lord. However, if you carefully read the part that says,
"*train up a child in the way he should go,*" a further truth
begins to emerge. Parenting isn't only about teaching
children in the ways of the Lord, but their responsibility
is also to train them "*in the way he* [the child] *should go.*"
The Amplified version says, "*Train up a child in the way
he should go [teaching him to seek God's wisdom and will*

for his abilities and talents]." True discipleship is about training and teaching the disciple to seek God's will and wisdom in order to discover their own specific purpose. Oftentimes, we disciple others according to our own desires, rather than guiding them in the path that God has designed for them.

We need to understand the importance of instructing the next generation to follow their own path according to the abilities and talents that God has placed in them. Otherwise, it may give birth to rebellion. To bring this into perspective, Jesus told Saul, "*Why are you persecuting Me? It is hard for you to kick against the goads*" (Acts 26:14b). A goad was a pointed piece of timber stick that was used to urge a stubborn ox to move. Figuratively speaking, we have placed goads in this generation, forcing them to walk our path and not the one they should go. Instead of discipling a generation we are hurting them and causing them to rebel. The Scripture says that John the Baptist was to "*Prepare the way of the LORD*" and "Make *His paths straigh*t" (Mark 1:3). We ought to be as John and help prepare the way for the generation after us. Let's look into some examples.

David and Solomon

King David was known as a man after God's heart. However, his reign of forty years in Israel was filled with wars and battles against the enemy. Although David shed much blood throughout his life, he didn't instruct Solomon to follow his path of war, but instead to build the temple of God, the path God had prepared for him. We're able to see how David set his kingdom in order before dying, giving instructions to Solomon pertaining to the kingdom he was handing over to him (see I Kings 2). David understood how to train up his son Solomon in the way that he was born to go. As a result, Solomon didn't have to fight any wars because his father David followed and fulfilled his destiny, while preparing the way for his son Solomon.

Moses and Joshua

Moses and the generation that crossed the Red Sea (except for Joshua and Caleb) didn't enter the Promised Land. However, Moses took it upon himself to teach the commandments of the Lord to the next generation. He selflessly passed the baton to Joshua, his successor, to finish the race and enter the Promised Land. We must understand that we might not see the fulfillment of every promise of God in our lifetime, but if we are faithful, our children and grandchildren will see it come to fruition. For example, God promised Abraham that he would become a great nation, yet he didn't see the promise fulfilled in its entirety throughout his lifetime. Remember, we aren't called to run an independent race, but a relay race. Let's disciple those following after us, teaching and training them in the way that they should go.

SERVANTHOOD

Another important key to true discipleship is servant-hood. The Scriptures have a lot to say about servanthood. Let's read Matthew 20:26-28 where Jesus spoke to His disciples concerning servanthood:

> 26 Yet it shall not be so among you; but whoever desires to become great among you, let him be your servant. 27 And whoever desires to be first among you, let him be your slave— 28 just as the Son of Man did not come to be served, but to serve, and to give His life a ransom for many."

Jesus explains that if a person desires to be great, he will have to first become a servant. He didn't only teach His disciples about the importance of serving, but He Himself, being God in the flesh, became a man, and washed His disciples' feet in order to teach them the principle of servanthood (see John 13:1-17). Paul wrote about Jesus in Philippians 2:6-7 saying,

> Who, being in the form of God, did not consider it robbery to be equal with God, but made Himself of

no reputation, taking the form of a bondservant, and coming in the likeness of men."

In this passage, Paul goes on to describe Jesus as being more than a servant. He described Him as a bondservant. In the 1828 Merriam Webster dictionary, a "servant" is defined as *one that serves others,*[1] while a "bondservant" is *one bound to service without wages.*[2] Jesus didn't serve us to receive any type of benefit, but rather, He did it because of His unconditional love for humanity. Servanthood isn't an obligation, it's a choice of living. Servanthood is a key that opens doors to greatness and is a fundamental prerequisite for leadership.

Elijah and Elisha

Elisha became the successor of the great prophet Elijah. Elisha requested a double portion of Elijah's spirit (see 2 Kings 2:9), and after Elijah was taken

> *Servanthood is a key that opens doors to greatness and is a fundamental prerequisite for leadership.*

by the Lord, Elisha received his mantle, symbolic of the double portion. The thought of a double portion in the Bible is one of a double blessing. It was commonly used in the Old Testament to refer to a double blessing, or to the birthright of a firstborn.

- *The Law of Moses used this term to describe the double portion assigned to the firstborn son* (Deuteronomy 21:17).

- *Elkanah gave his wife Hannah a double portion because of his love for her despite her barrenness* (1 Samuel 1:5).

- *Job received twice as much as he had before his trial* (Job 42:10).

Interestingly, the Scripture records that Elisha performed twice as many miracles than Elijah had. So, what was the key to Elisha's double portion? It was his spirit of servanthood. How many people had prayed to the Lord for a "double portion"? It may sound very spiritual, however, a double portion isn't received by the laying on of hands, or by anointing with oil. Elisha had the right to receive a double portion due to all his years of service. He served faithfully in another man's ministry, giving him the right to ask and receive a double portion. Jesus' disciples performed great signs, miracles, and wonders because they served Him. Discipleship implies that you have a heart to serve others.

DECREASE

Another fundamental key is the act of conceding. John the Baptist told His disciples that, *"He [Jesus] must increase, but I must decrease"* (John 3:30). Before Jesus was baptized in the Jordan River and began His ministry, John the Baptist was a famous preacher, well known throughout Israel. The crowd went to him to hear the message of repentance and to be baptized in water. Then, when the ministry of Jesus began, the people started going to Jesus instead to be baptized and discipled by Him. Some of the disciples that remained in John's ministry asked John, "*Rabbi, He who was with you beyond the Jordan, to whom you have testified—behold, He is baptizing, and all are coming to Him!*" (John 3:26). John's disciples wanted answers as to why everyone was leaving to follow Jesus' ministry. John the Baptist didn't criticize or speak evil against Jesus and His ministry, but instead he said, "*He must increase, but I must decrease*" (John 3:30). John understood that it was time to pass the baton, and that meant to humbly concede his ministry to its rightful successor. There was no envy or hatred in John's heart, hence his confession in verse 29, "*Therefore this joy of mine is fulfilled.*" John was joyful and fulfilled, not only because he accomplished his earthly assignment, but also because he successfully passed the baton. Likewise, in the relay race, after having run his distance, the runner needs to transition and pass the baton to the next runner, successfully. There will be a transition in our lives where we'll have to decrease (move out of the way) and allow the generation after us to increase (step into their destiny). Jesus, being God, humbled Himself by becoming a man and ascended to heaven so we may continue His great work on earth as His body.

PATERNITY

In my opinion, the number one issue in this generation is the lack of fathers. The lack of fathers isn't only a spiritual crisis in the church, but an epidemic in the United States. "The Fatherless Generation"[3] quotes some disturbing statistics of fatherless children in the U.S.:

- *63% of youth suicides are from fatherless homes.*
- *71% of all high school dropouts come from fatherless homes.*
- *90% of all homeless and runaway children are from fatherless homes.*
- *85% of all youths in prison come from fatherless homes.*

It's heart breaking to know how we, the Church, have allowed the enemy to infiltrate our homes and bring destruction. The Scripture clearly says that *"if a house is divided against itself, that house cannot stand"* (Mark 3:25). The foundation of a house is the most important part of its construction. The foundation is created to withstand the weight of a house, and a house without a strong foundation won't stand. Likewise, a father is the foundation of a household. Fathers withhold the weight of the family. The enemy knows that if he can destroy the head (the father figure) in the family, he can destroy a generation.

Father Versus Teacher

Paul wrote, *"For though you might have ten thousand instructors in Christ, yet you do not have many fathers"* (1 Corinthians 4:15a). Nowadays, there are thousands and thousands of teachers of the Word of God. If you search YouTube or the Internet, you will find yourself with a ton of knowledge and information on the subject. However, the nation lacks fathers. In order to understand this truth, we must understand the difference between a father and a teacher.

Let's first look at the responsibility of a teacher. A teacher is responsible to expand a student's knowledge and provide information in a specific subject. According to the knowledge a student receives, the student is tested accordingly. The test determines whether the student is able to pass the class. The objective of the instructor isn't to concern themself with the personal life of the students (though they might care), their duty is to expand the student's knowledge.

Whereas a father's goals and priorities transcend that of an instructor (though important to him), his objective is to also care about his children and to be constantly involved in his child's personal life. He knows when his child is sick, needs a hug or a kiss, needs time alone, and so on. He's responsible for building character in the child's life. A teacher provides knowledge, but a father builds character and brings restoration.

Let's look at a simple illustration. Pedro is struggling with depression and suicidal thoughts

> *A teacher provides knowledge, but a father builds character and brings restoration.*

and his condition is affecting his academic grades. A teacher is responsible for Pedro's grades and his focus is to help Pedro pass the class. Whatever happens outside of Pedro's academia isn't his responsibility. A teacher evaluates students according to their academic performance. However, a parent is responsible for his children's personal life and their restoration. Teachers are extremely important for this generation because they bring growth. However, what this generation is lacking is character, and there is a lack of character because there is a lack of fathers. For this reason, we must pray that the hearts of the fathers return to their children, and in turn, the hearts of the children to their fathers (see Malachi 4:6).

Generation to Generations

God isn't looking for *a* generation, but rather for *the* generation in which to release His glory. It's not only about releasing the glory of God in our lives, but also about instructing and helping the generation after us to release His glory as well. Are we willing to be like our brother Stephen, who was willing to be stoned so Paul could rise? We must be willing to die to ourselves that others after us may rise. This isn't about me, myself, and I, but about our LORD Jesus Christ, and His body working together as one. Do you know what it means to finish the race? It's not only to accomplish your assignment or purpose on earth, but also that what the LORD began in you may continue after you and bring expansion of God's Kingdom here on earth. Passing the baton successfully opens the gateway for greater glory to be released on the earth. May those who run after us release a greater glory in Christ's name.

<u>RELAY RACE</u>

The purpose of this chapter is to demonstrate what true discipleship entails and why it is important to pass successful discipleship to our next generation.

REVIEW QUESTIONS

1. According to Proverbs 22:6, how you will train up a child?

    _____

    _____

    _____

2. Read Matthew 20:26-28 and write how being great relates to being a servant.

    _____

    _____

    _____

3. In your own words, explain Malachi 4:6.

    _____

    _____

    _____

    _____

PERSONAL QUESTIONS

1. What kind of legacy do you want to leave after you die?

   _____

   _____

2. Did you grow without a father? If yes, how did that affect you growing up?

   _____

   _____

3. How important is a spiritual father in your life?

   _____

   _____

Prayer Time: Let's take a moment and pray that we may successfully pass our baton to the generation that follows us. (Read II Kings 2:9-13.)

Heavenly Father,

I pray not only that You help to accomplish Your purpose on earth and release Your glory, but also that I may pass the baton to the next generation successfully that they would do greater work than I did, and they will reveal the fullness of Your glory on earth. In the precious name of Jesus Christ I pray.

Amen

Conclusion

Churches have been waiting for centuries for God's glory to be revealed on earth. But it is up to us, His chosen generation, to bring God's glory to the world. As I close this book, I want to encourage everyone to start releasing God's glory by applying these key principles in their lives. You were chosen by God not to simply be dust, but to release His glory. As you walk in alignment with God's purpose for your life and use what He has given you, His glory will be released. He waits for you to shine His bright light in the midst of darkness. As Jesus said, "*A city on a hill cannot be hidden*" (Matthew 5:14). Let us begin our journey to become a Chosen Generation, as we shine His bright light to the world. Never give up, stay strong and encourage one another, so that this generation will turn the world upside down, hastening the coming of Jesus.

KNOWING YOURSELF PERSONAL QUESTIONNAIRE

Answer the following questions to help you begin to know yourself better:

1. What are some of your strengths?

    _____

    _____

    _____

2. What are some of your weaknesses?

    _____

    _____

    _____

3. What brings out the worst side of you?

    _____

    _____

    _____

4. What brings out the best side of you?

    _____

    _____

    _____

5. How would you describe yourself in one single word?

   _____

6. What are some characteristics or traits that describe you?

   _____

   _____

   _____

7. What qualities do you have that make you unique from everyone else?

   _____

   _____

   _____

8. What do you love the most about yourself?

   _____

   _____

   _____

9. What do you hate the most about yourself?

   _____

   _____

   _____

10. Are you an introvert or extrovert?

   _____

11. Are you more likely to avoid conflict or engage in it head-on?

_____

_____

_____

12. What things in life make you the happiest?

_____

_____

_____

13. What is in your life that you want to improve upon?

_____

_____

_____

14. Describe yourself in one paragraph.

_____

_____

_____

_____

_____

_____

15. What do you enjoy or love to do?

_____

_____

_____

16. How do you like to relax?

_____

_____

_____

17. What activities make you lose track of time?

_____

_____

_____

18. Where do you seem to have the most influence?

_____

_____

_____

19. What do you consider to be some of your gifts?

_____

_____

_____

20. What is your dream vacation?

_____

_____

_____

21. What did you like to do as a child?

_____

_____

_____

22. What were your nicknames growing up, and why?

_____

_____

_____

23. Is your nickname applicable to you today?

_____

24. If you could create your dream job, what would it be?

_____

_____

_____

25. If you had all the time in the world, what else would you be doing?

_____

_____

_____

26. If money were no longer an issue, what would you spend the rest of your life doing?

_____

_____

_____

27. What areas of your life come easy to you that most people find to be a struggle?

_____

_____

_____

28. How would your closest friends and family members describe you?

_____

_____

_____

29. In what area do you tend to get the most compliments from others?

_____

_____

_____

30. After you die, what legacy do you want to leave on the earth?

_____

_____

_____

31. What do you want to be the last words to your family before you die?

_____

_____

_____

32. How would you impact generations?

_____

_____

_____

_____

33. Is there something you want to learn more about?

_____

_____

_____

34. Name three heroes or role models in your life and why they are they your hero or role model.

_____

_____

_____

35. What do you see yourself doing 10 years from now?

_____

_____

_____

36. What is your favorite subject and why?

_____

_____

_____

37. If you had only 10 years to live, what would you being doing before you die?

_____

_____

_____

38. What is your greatest fear?

_____

_____

39. What are you most grateful for in your life?

_____

_____

_____

40. What is the most important lesson you've learned in your life?

_____

_____

_____

41. Is there one job you will never ever do?

_____

_____

_____

42. What does it mean to you to make a difference in the world?

_____

_____

_____

_____

43. What are you most thankful for in life?

_____

_____

_____

_____

44. How would you define success? What is a successful life to you? Describe it in your own words.

_____

_____

_____

_____

_____

45. What do you think of your generation?

_____

_____

_____

46. What do you think of the next generation?

_____

_____

_____

47. What will people say about you at your funeral?

_____

_____

_____

48. What is the purpose of life?

_____

_____

_____

49. What is your life vision?

_____

_____

_____

50. Describe your life in one word?

_____

Reflection: The main reason for asking these questions is to challenge yourself to look deep into what the LORD has placed inside of you. Many times, we spend years occupied with work, family, ministry, or other things, and we forget to spend time knowing ourselves and the gifts God has placed in us. There are dreams and visions that have been dormant in your life and are waiting to be awakened, and the only thing preventing you from fulfilling it is yourself, fear of failure, or maybe feeling too comfortable with where you are. Today, it's time to get up and take a leap of faith by trusting in the LORD with all of your heart.

Endnotes

Introduction

1. "H3520 - kabod - Strong's Hebrew Lexicon (nkjv)." Blue Letter Bible. Accessed July 12, 2021. https://www. blueletterbible.org/lexicon/h3520/nkjv/wlc/0-1/.

2. "H3335 - yasar - Strong's Hebrew Lexicon (nkjv)." Blue Letter Bible. Web. Accessed June 23, 2021. https:// www.blueletterbible.org/lexicon/h3520/nkjv/wlc/0-1/.

Chapter 1

1. "G1097 - ginosko - Strong's Greek Lexicon (NKJV)." Blue Letter Bible. Web. May 14, 2020. https://www. blueletterbible.org/lexicon/g1097/nkjv/tr/0-1/.

Chapter 2

1. "H3091 - yeshua - Strong's Hebrew Lexicon (NKJV)." Blue Letter Bible. Accessed August 21, 2021. https:// www.blueletterbible.org/lexicon/h3091/nkjv/wlc/0-1/.

Chapter 3

1. "H6754 - selem - Strong's Hebrew Lexicon (NKJV)." Blue Letter Bible. Web. July 23, 2021. https://www. blueletterbible.org/lexicon/h6754/nkjv/wlc/0-1/.

2. "H6738 - sel - Strong's Hebrew Lexicon (NKJV)." Blue Letter Bible. Web. July 23, 2021. https://www.blueletterbible.org/lexicon/h6738/nkjv/wlc/0-1/.

3. "Shadow." Merriam-Webster. 2020. https://www. merriam-webster.com (accessed May 14, 2020).

4. "H6942 - qadash - Strong's Hebrew Lexicon (NKJV)." Blue Letter Bible. Web. Accessed July 23, 2021. https://www.blueletterbible.org/lexicon/h6942/nkjv/wlc/0-1/.

5. "Communion." Noah Webster's Dictionary 1828. 2020. http: //webstersdictionary1828.com (accessed May 20, 2020).

6. "H4397 - malak - Strong's Hebrew Lexicon (NKJV)." Blue Letter Bible. Web. Accessed July 23, 2021. https://www.blueletterbible.org/lexicon/h4397/nkjv/wlc/0-1/.

7. "G32 - angelos - Strong's Greek Lexicon (NKJV)." Blue Letter Bible. Web. Accessed July 23, 2021. https://www.blueletterbible.org/lexicon/g32/nkjv/tr/0-1/.

Chapter 4

1. Wachowski, Andy, Larry Wachowski, Keanu Reeves, Laurence Fishburne, and Carrie-Anne Moss. *The Matrix*. Burbank, CA: Warner Home Video, 1999.

Chapter 5

1. "Identity." Merriam-Webster. 2020. https://www.merriam-webster.com (accessed May 15, 2020).
2. "Identity theft." Merriam-Webster. 2020.https://www.merriam-webster.com (accessed May 15, 2020).
3. P, Kim. "23 College Dropout Statistics That Will Surprise You." CreditDonkey, November 12, 2019. www.creditdonkey.com/college-dropout-statistics.html.
4. Plumer, Brad. "Only 27 Percent of College Grads Have a Job Related to Their Major." The Washington Post, May 20, 2013. https://www.washingtonpost.com/news/wonk/wp/2013/05/20/only-27-percent-of-college-grads-have-a-job-related-to-their-major/
5. Lieberman, Lexi. "Still Undecided? Here's How To Pick Your College Major." Study Break, August 24, 2017. studybreaks.com/college/undecided-how-to-pick-college-major/.
6. Wallnau, L. (2013). The Seven Mountain Strategy: Journey to Convergence. International School of

Ministry: Maturity Module (p. 9). Student Workbook, Good Shepherd Ministries.

7. "G5486 - charisma - Strong's Greek Lexicon (NKJV)." Blue Letter Bible. Accessed August 28, 2021.https://www.blueletterbible.org/lexicon/g5486/nkjv/tr/0-1/.

8. "Gift." Merriam-Webster. 2020.https://www.merriam-webster.com (May 15, 2020).

9. Myles Munroe (2010). "Kingdom Principles Trade Paper: Preparing for Kingdom Experience and Expansion." Pg. 3. ReadHowYouWant.com.

Chapter 6

1. David Yong-gi Cho, Preface, The Fourth Dimension (Vol 1), Published: US, Bridge-Logos Publishers, 1979. Pg 1.

Chapter 7

1. Cho, Dr. David Yonggi. *Successful Home Cell Groups*. Bridge-Logos, 1987.

2. "Tracy McGrady: Kobe Bryant Used To Say 'I Want To Die Young.'" YouTube. uploaded by ClutchPoints. January 7, 2020. https://youtube/mpHRSovRMrk.

3. "Blueprint." Merriam-Webster. 2020. https://www.merriam-webster.com (May 15, 2020).

4. "Extraordinary." Merriam-Webster. 2020. https://www.merriam-webster.com (May 15, 2020).

5. "H3876 - Lowt - Strong's Hebrew Lexicon (KJV)." Blue Letter Bible. Web. June 7, 2020. https://www.blueletterbible.org//lang/lexicon/lexicon.cfm?Strongs=H3876&t=KJV.

6. "Eternity." Lexico Dictionaries. 2020. https://www.lexico.com (May 15, 2020).

7. "Eternity." dictionary.com. 2020. https://www.dictionary.com (May 15, 2020).

8. "G1097 - ginosko - Strong's Greek Lexicon (NKJV)." Blue Letter Bible. Web. May 14, 2020. https://www.blueletterbible.org//lang/lexicon/lexicon.cfm?Strongs=G1097&t=NKJV.

Chapter 9

1. David Mikkelson, "Dr. Howard Kelly and the Glass of Milk." Snopes, September 13, 2013. www.snopes.com/fact-check/the-milk-of-human-kindness/.

2. Mendoza-Moyers, Diego. "Yes, More of Your Fruits and Veggies Are from Overseas." Times Union, April 13, 2019. www.timesunion.com/business/article/Yes-more-of-the-fruits-and-vegetables-you-re-13762595.php.

Chapter 10

1. "Servant." Merriam-Webster. 2020. https://www.merriam-webster.com (May 14, 2020).

2. "Bondservant." Merriam-Webster. 2020. https://www.merriam-webster.com (May 14, 2020).

3. Sabrina. "The Fatherless Generation." April 23, 2010, https://thefatherlessgeneration.wordpress.com

Made in the USA
Middletown, DE
13 March 2022

62462256R00137